MznLnx

Missing Links Exam Preps

Exam Prep for

Principles of Finance

Beasley & Brigham, 3rd Edition

The MznLnx Exam Prep is your link from the texbook and lecture to your exams.
The MznLnx Exam Preps are unauthorized and comprehensive reviews of your textbooks.

MznLnx

Rico
Publications

Exam Prep for Principles of Finance
3rd Edition
Beasley & Brigham

Publisher: Raymond Houge
Assistant Editor: Michael Rouger
Text and Cover Designer: Lisa Buckner
Marketing Manager: Sara Swagger
Project Manager, Editorial Production: Jerry Emerson
Art Director: Vernon Lowerui
Product Manager: Dave Mason
Editorial Assitant: Rachel Guzmanji
Pedagogy: Debra Long
Cover Image: Jim Reed/Getty Images
Text and Cover Printer: City Printing, Inc.
Compositor: Media Mix, Inc.

Printed in the United States
ISBN:

For more information about our products, contact us at:
Dave.Mason@RicoPublications.com

For permission to use material from this text or product, submit a request online to:
Dave.Mason@RicoPublications.com

Contents

TO THE STUDENT

COMPREHENSIVE

The *MznLnx* Exam Prep series is designed to help you pass your exams. Editors at MznLnx review your textbooks and then prepare these practice exams to help you master the textbook material. Unlike study guides, workbooks, and practice tests provided by the texbook publisher and textbook authors, *MznLnx* gives you ***all*** of the material in each chapter in exam form, not just samples, so you can be sure to nail your exam.

MECHANICAL

The MznLnx Exam Prep series creates exams that will help you learn the subject matter as well as test you on your understanding. Each question is designed to help you master the concept. Just working through the exams, you gain an understanding of the subject--its a simple mechanical process that produces success.

INTEGRATED STUDY GUIDE AND REVIEW

MznLnx is not just a set of exams designed to test you, its also a comprehensive review of the subject content. Each exam question is also a review of the concept, making sure that you will get the answer correct without having to go to other sources of material. You learn as you go! Its the easiest way to pass an exam.

HUMOR

Studying can be tedious and dry. MznLnx's instructional design includes moderate humor within the exam questions on occassion, to break the tedium and revitalize the brain

1. In finance, _________ (or gearing) is borrowing money to supplement existing funds for investment in such a way that the potential positive or negative outcome is magnified and/or enhanced. It generally refers to using borrowed funds, or debt, so as to attempt to increase the returns to equity. Deleveraging is the action of reducing borrowings.
   a. Limited partnership
   b. Financial endowment
   c. Pension fund
   d. Leverage

2. The phrase _________ refers to the aspect of corporate strategy, corporate finance and management dealing with the buying, selling and combining of different companies that can aid, finance, or help a growing company in a given industry grow rapidly without having to create another business entity.

An acquisition, also known as a takeover, is the buying of one company (the 'target') by another. An acquisition may be friendly or hostile.

   a. 529 plan
   b. Mergers and acquisitions
   c. 7-Eleven
   d. 4-4-5 Calendar

3. A _________ is a professionally managed type of collective investment scheme that pools money from many investors and invests it in stocks, bonds, short-term money market instruments, and/or other securities. The _________ will have a fund manager that trades the pooled money on a regular basis. Currently, the worldwide value of all _________s totals more than $26 trillion.

Since 1940, there have been three basic types of investment companies in the United States: open-end funds, also known in the US as _________s; unit investment trusts (UITs); and closed-end funds.

   a. Net asset value
   b. Trust company
   c. Mutual fund
   d. Financial intermediary

4. _________ is a financial metric which represents operating liquidity available to a business. Along with fixed assets such as plant and equipment, _________ is considered a part of operating capital. It is calculated as current assets minus current liabilities.

a. 4-4-5 Calendar
b. Working capital management
c. 529 plan
d. Working capital

5. A _________ is a private or public market for the trading of company stock and derivatives of company stock at an agreed price; these are securities listed on a stock exchange as well as those only traded privately.

The size of the world _________ is estimated at about $36.6 trillion US at the beginning of October 2008 . The world derivatives market has been estimated at about $480 trillion face or nominal value, 12 times the size of the entire world economy.

a. Adolph Coors
b. Anton Gelonkin
c. Stock market
d. Andrew Tobias

6. A _________ is a sudden dramatic decline of stock prices across a significant cross-section of a stock market. Crashes are driven by panic as much as by underlying economic factors. They often follow speculative stock market bubbles.
a. 7-Eleven
b. 529 plan
c. 4-4-5 Calendar
d. Stock market crash

7. A _________ or equity fund is a fund that invests in Equities more commonly known as stocks. Such funds are typically held either in stock or cash, as opposed to Bonds, notes, or other securities. This may be a mutual fund or exchange-traded fund.
a. Stock fund
b. Money market funds
c. Closed-end fund
d. Mutual fund fees and expenses

8. _________ is a measure of the ability of a debtor to pay their debts as and when they fall due. It is usually expressed as a ratio or a percentage of current liabilities.

For a corporation with a published balance sheet there are various ratios used to calculate a measure of liquidity.

a. Invested capital
b. Operating leverage
c. Operating profit margin
d. Accounting liquidity

9. A _________ occurs when a financial sponsor acquires a controlling interest in a company's equity and where a significant percentage of the purchase price is financed through leverage (borrowing.) The assets of the acquired company are used as collateral for the borrowed capital, sometimes with assets of the acquiring company. The bonds or other paper issued for _________s are commonly considered not to be investment grade because of the significant risks involved.

a. Leveraged buyout
b. Limited partnership
c. Leverage
d. Pension fund

10. _________ is the removal or simplification of government rules and regulations that constrain the operation of market forces. _________ does not mean elimination of laws against fraud, but eliminating or reducing government control of how business is done, thereby moving toward a more free market.

The stated rationale for '_________' is often that fewer and simpler regulations will lead to a raised level of competitiveness, therefore higher productivity, more efficiency and lower prices overall.

a. Demand shock
b. Value added
c. Supply shock
d. Deregulation

1. The institution most often referenced by the word '_________' is a public or publicly traded _________, the shares of which are traded on a public stock exchange (e.g., the New York Stock Exchange or Nasdaq in the United States) where shares of stock of _________s are bought and sold by and to the general public. Most of the largest businesses in the world are publicly traded _________s. However, the majority of _________s are said to be closely held, privately held or close _________s, meaning that no ready market exists for the trading of shares.

a. Protect
b. Federal Home Loan Mortgage Corporation
c. Depository Trust Company
d. Corporation

2. _________ is that which is owed; usually referencing assets owed, but the term can cover other obligations. In the case of assets, _________ is a means of using future purchasing power in the present before a summation has been earned. Some companies and corporations use _________ as a part of their overall corporate finance strategy.

a. Cross-collateralization
b. Partial Payment
c. Credit cycle
d. Debt

3. _________, in finance and accounting, means stated value or face value. From this comes the expressions at par (at the _________), over par (over _________) and under par (under _________.)

The term '_________' has several meanings depending on context and geography.

a. Par value
b. Global Squeeze
c. FIDC
d. Sinking fund

4. In accounting, _________ refers to the portion of net income which is retained by the corporation rather than distributed to its owners as dividends. Similarly, if the corporation makes a loss, then that loss is retained and called variously retained losses, accumulated losses or accumulated deficit. _________ and losses are cumulative from year to year with losses offsetting earnings.

a. Generally Accepted Accounting Principles
b. Historical cost
c. Matching principle
d. Retained earnings

5. _________ is a fee paid on borrowed assets. It is the price paid for the use of borrowed money , or, money earned by deposited funds . Assets that are sometimes lent with _________ include money, shares, consumer goods through hire purchase, major assets such as aircraft, and even entire factories in finance lease arrangements.

a. A Random Walk Down Wall Street
b. AAB
c. Insolvency
d. Interest

6. _________ is a life of security. It may also refer to the final payment date of a loan or other financial instrument, at which point all remaining interest and principal is due to be paid.

1, 3, 6 months _________ band can be calculated by using 30-day per month periods.

a. Replacement cost
b. Primary market
c. False billing
d. Maturity

7. A _________ is a fungible, negotiable instrument representing financial value. They are broadly categorized into debt securities (such as banknotes, bonds and debentures), and equity securities; e.g., common stocks. The company or other entity issuing the _________ is called the issuer.

a. Tracking stock
b. Securities lending
c. Book entry
d. Security

8. In finance, the term _________ describes the amount in cash that returns to the owners of a security. Normally it does not include the price variations, at the difference of the total return. _________ applies to various stated rates of return on stocks (common and preferred, and convertible), fixed income instruments (bonds, notes, bills, strips, zero coupon), and some other investment type insurance products (e.g. annuities.)

a. Macaulay duration
b. Yield
c. 4-4-5 Calendar
d. Yield to maturity

9. In the United States, _________ are overnight borrowings by banks to maintain their bank reserves at the Federal Reserve. Banks keep reserves at Federal Reserve Banks to meet their reserve requirements and to clear financial transactions. Transactions in the _________ market enable depository institutions with reserve balances in excess of reserve requirements to lend reserves to institutions with reserve deficiencies.

a. Federal funds rate
b. 4-4-5 Calendar
c. Regulation T
d. Federal funds

10. The phrase _________ refers to the aspect of corporate strategy, corporate finance and management dealing with the buying, selling and combining of different companies that can aid, finance, or help a growing company in a given industry grow rapidly without having to create another business entity.

An acquisition, also known as a takeover, is the buying of one company (the 'target') by another. An acquisition may be friendly or hostile.

a. Mergers and acquisitions
b. 4-4-5 Calendar
c. 529 plan
d. 7-Eleven

11. A _________ allows a borrower to use a financial security as collateral for a cash loan at a fixed rate of interest. In a repo, the borrower agrees to immediately sell a security to a lender and also agrees to buy the same security from the lender at a fixed price at some later date. A repo is equivalent to a cash transaction combined with a forward contract.

a. Volatility arbitrage
b. Total return swap
c. Contango
d. Repurchase agreement

12. _________ mature in one year or less. Like zero-coupon bonds, they do not pay interest prior to maturity; instead they are sold at a discount of the par value to create a positive yield to maturity. Many regard _________ as the least risky investment available to U.S. investors.

a. 4-4-5 Calendar
b. Treasury securities
c. Treasury Inflation Protected Securities
d. Treasury bills

13. A _________ s a time deposit, a financial product commonly offered to consumers by banks, thrift institutions, and credit unions.

They are similar to savings accounts in that they are insured and thus virtually risk-free; they are 'money in the bank'. They are different from savings accounts in that they have a specific, fixed term (often three months, six months, or one to five years), and, usually, a fixed interest rate.

a. Certificate of Deposit
b. Reserve requirement
c. Time deposit
d. Variable rate mortgage

14. _________ is the removal or simplification of government rules and regulations that constrain the operation of market forces. _________ does not mean elimination of laws against fraud, but eliminating or reducing government control of how business is done, thereby moving toward a more free market.

The stated rationale for '_________' is often that fewer and simpler regulations will lead to a raised level of competitiveness, therefore higher productivity, more efficiency and lower prices overall.

a. Demand shock
b. Supply shock
c. Deregulation
d. Value added

15. _________s are deposits denominated in United States dollars at banks outside the United States, and thus are not under the jurisdiction of the Federal Reserve. Consequently, such deposits are subject to much less regulation than similar deposits within the United States, allowing for higher margins. There is nothing 'European' about _________ deposits; a US dollar-denominated deposit in Tokyo or Caracas would likewise be deemed _________ deposits.

a. A Random Walk Down Wall Street
b. ABN Amro
c. AAB
d. Eurodollar

16. _________ is the term used to describe deposits residing in banks that are located outside the borders of the country that issues the currency the deposit is denominated in. For example a deposit denominated in US dollars residing in a Japanese bank is a _________ deposit, or more specifically a Eurodollar deposit.

Key points are the location of the bank and the denomination of the currency, not the nationality of the bank or the owner of the deposit/loan.

a. ABN Amro
b. A Random Walk Down Wall Street
c. Eurocurrency
d. AAB

17. A _________ is a professionally managed type of collective investment scheme that pools money from many investors and invests it in stocks, bonds, short-term money market instruments, and/or other securities. The _________ will have a fund manager that trades the pooled money on a regular basis. Currently, the worldwide value of all _________s totals more than $26 trillion.

Since 1940, there have been three basic types of investment companies in the United States: open-end funds, also known in the US as _________s; unit investment trusts (UITs); and closed-end funds.

a. Trust company
b. Net asset value
c. Mutual fund
d. Financial intermediary

18. In finance, a _________ is a debt security, in which the authorized issuer owes the holders a debt and, depending on the terms of the _________, is obliged to pay interest (the coupon) and/or to repay the principal at a later date, termed maturity.

Thus a _________ is a loan: the issuer is the borrower, the _________ holder is the lender, and the coupon is the interest. _________s provide the borrower with external funds to finance long-term investments, or, in the case of government _________s, to finance current expenditure.

a. Puttable bond
b. Convertible bond
c. Catastrophe bonds
d. Bond

19. A _________ is a legal pledge in United States municipal finance, in which an entity pledges its full faith and credit to repay its debt, typically a _________ bond.

a. Letter of credit
b. Financial Institutions Reform Recovery and Enforcement Act
c. General obligation
d. Covenant

20. A _________ is a bond issued by a national government denominated in the country's own currency. Bonds issued by national governments in foreign currencies are normally referred to as sovereign bonds. The first ever _________ was issued by the British government in 1693 to raise money to fund a war against France.

a. Zero-coupon bond
b. Government bond
c. Municipal bond
d. Collateralized debt obligations

21. In the United States, a _________ is a bond issued by a city or other local government, or their agencies. Potential issuers of these bonds include cities, counties, redevelopment agencies, school districts, publicly owned airports and seaports, and any other governmental entity (or group of governments) below the state level. They may be general obligations of the issuer or secured by specified revenues.

a. Premium bond
b. Senior debt
c. Puttable bond
d. Municipal bond

22. In business, _________ is income that a company receives from its normal business activities, usually from the sale of goods and services to customers. Some companies also receive _________ from interest, dividends or royalties paid to them by other companies. _________ may refer to business income in general, or it may refer to the amount, in a monetary unit, received during a period of time, as in 'Last year, Company X had _________ of $32 million.'

In many countries, including the UK, _________ is referred to as turnover.

a. Furniture, Fixtures and Equipment
b. Matching principle
c. Revenue
d. Bottom line

23. _________ are bonds issued by governments, authorities, or public benefit corporations that are guaranteed by the revenue flow of the issuing agency.

The Supreme Court decision of Pollock versus Farmer's Loan and Trust Company of 1895 initiated a wave or series of innovations for the financial services community in both tax-treatment and regulation from government. This specific case, according to a leading investment bank's research, resulted in the 'intergovernmental tax immunity doctrine,' ultimately leading to 'tax-free status.' Municipal bonds are generally exempt from federal tax on their interest payments (not capital gains.)

a. Callable bond
b. Gilts
c. Private activity bond
d. Revenue bonds

24. A _________ is defined as a certificate of agreement of loans which is given under the company's stamp and carries an undertaking that the _________ holder will get a fixed return (fixed on the basis of interest rates) and the principal amount whenever the _________ matures.

In finance, a _________ is a long-term debt instrument used by governments and large companies to obtain funds. It is defined as 'a debt secured only by the debtor's earning power, not by a lien on any specific asset.' It is similar to a bond except the securitization conditions are different.

a. Partial Payment
b. Collection agency
c. Collateral Management
d. Debenture

25. In finance, a _________ (non-investment grade bond, speculative grade bond or junk bond) is a bond that is rated below investment grade at the time of purchase. These bonds have a higher risk of default or other adverse credit events, but typically pay higher yields than better quality bonds in order to make them attractive to investors.

a. High yield bond
b. Private equity
c. Sharpe ratio
d. Volatility

26. _________ is a combination of straight bond and embedded put option. The holder of the _________ has the right, but not the obligation, to demand early repayment of the principal. The put option is usually exercisable on specified dates.

a. Brady bonds
b. Puttable bond
c. Convertible bond
d. Callable bond

27. A _________ is a fund established by a government agency or business for the purpose of reducing debt.

The _________ was first used in Great Britain in the 18th century to reduce national debt. While used by Robert Walpole in 1716 and effectively in the 1720s and early 1730s, it originated in the commercial tax syndicates of the Italian peninsula of the 14th century to retire redeemable public debt of those cities.

a. Security interest
b. Debtor
c. Modern portfolio theory
d. Sinking fund

28. A _________, in its most general sense, is a solemn promise to engage in or refrain from a specified action.

More specifically, a _________, in contrast to a contract, is a one-way agreement whereby the _________er is the only party bound by the promise. A _________ may have conditions and prerequisites that qualify the undertaking, including the actions of second or third parties, but there is no inherent agreement by such other parties to fulfill those requirements.

a. Federal Trade Commission Act
b. Partnership
c. Clayton Antitrust Act
d. Covenant

29. In financial accounting, _________s are precautions for which the amount or probability of occurrence are not known. Typical examples are _________s for warranty costs and _________ for taxes the term reserve is used instead of term _________; such a use, however, is inconsistent with the terminology suggested by International Accounting Standards Board.
a. Money measurement concept
b. Petty cash
c. Momentum Accounting and Triple-Entry Bookkeeping
d. Provision

30. _________ are those dividends paid out in form of additional stock shares of the issuing corporation or other corporation They are usually issued in proportion to shares owned (for example for every 100 shares of stock owned, 5% stock dividend will yield 5 extra shares). If this payment involves the issue of new shares, this is very similar to a stock split in that it increases the total number of shares while lowering the price of each share and does not change the market capitalization or the total value of the shares held
a. Time-based currency
b. Database auditing
c. The Hong Kong Securities Institute
d. Stock or scrip dividends

31. A _________ is a payment made by a corporation to its shareholder members. When a corporation earns a profit or surplus, that money can be put to two uses: it can either be re-invested in the business (called retained earnings), or it can be paid to the shareholders as a _________. Many corporations retain a portion of their earnings and pay the remainder as a _________.

a. Special dividend
b. Dividend
c. Dividend yield
d. Dividend puzzle

32. The _________ on a company stock is the company's annual dividend payments divided by its market cap, or the dividend per share divided by the price per share. It is often expressed as a percentage.

Dividend payments on preferred shares are stipulated by the prospectus.

a. Dividend imputation
b. Dividend reinvestment plan
c. Special dividend
d. Dividend yield

33. _________ is typically a higher ranking stock than voting shares, and its terms are negotiated between the corporation and the investor.

_________ usually carry no voting rights, but may carry superior priority over common stock in the payment of dividends and upon liquidation. _________ may carry a dividend that is paid out prior to any dividends to common stock holders.

a. Follow-on offering
b. Second lien loan
c. Trade-off theory
d. Preferred stock

34. A mutual shareholder or _________ is an individual or company (including a corporation) that legally owns one or more shares of stock in a joint stock company. A company's shareholders collectively own that company. Thus, the typical goal of such companies is to enhance shareholder value.

a. Stock market bubble
b. Stockholder
c. Trading curb
d. Limit order

35. In business and finance, a _________ (also referred to as equity _________) of stock means a _________ of ownership in a corporation (company.) In the plural, stocks is often used as a synonym for _________s especially in the United States, but it is less commonly used that way outside of North America.

In the United Kingdom, South Africa, and Australia, stock can also refer to completely different financial instruments such as government bonds or, less commonly, to all kinds of marketable securities.

a. Share
b. Procter ' Gamble
c. Margin
d. Bucket shop

36. In business, a _________ is the purchase of one company (the target) by another (the acquirer or bidder). In the UK the term refers to the acquisition of a public company whose shares are listed on a stock exchange, in contrast to the acquisition of a private company.

Before a bidder makes an offer for another company, it usually first informs that company's board of directors.

a. Stock swap
b. 4-4-5 Calendar
c. Takeover
d. 529 plan

37. A _________ is a right to acquire certain property in preference to any other person. It usually refers to property newly coming into existence. A right to acquire existing property in preference to any other person is usually referred to as a right of first refusal.

In practice, the most common form of _________ is the right of existing shareholders to acquire newly issued shares issued by a company in a rights issue, a usually but not always public offering.

a. Down payment
b. Court of Audit of Belgium
c. Fraud deterrence
d. Pre-emption right

38. A _________ is a financial contract whose value is derived from the value of something else (known as the underlying.) The underlying on which a _________ is based can be an asset, weather conditions bonds or other forms of credit.

a. Derivative
b. 4-4-5 Calendar
c. 7-Eleven
d. 529 plan

39. An _________ is a contract written by a seller that conveys to the buyer the right -- but not the obligation -- to buy (in the case of a call _________) or to sell (in the case of a put _________) a particular asset, such as a piece of property such as, among others, a futures contract. In return for granting the _________, the seller collects a payment (the premium) from the buyer.

For example, buying a call _________ provides the right to buy a specified quantity of a security at a set strike price at some time on or before expiration, while buying a put _________ provides the right to sell.

a. Annuity
b. Amortization
c. Option
d. AT'T Mobility LLC

40. A _________ is a financial contract between two parties, the seller (writer) and the buyer of the option. The put allows its buyer the right but not the obligation to sell a commodity or financial instrument (the underlying instrument) to the writer (seller) of the option at a certain time for a certain price (the strike price.) The writer (seller) has the obligation to purchase the underlying asset at that strike price, if the buyer exercises the option.

a. Bear call spread
b. Bear spread
c. Put option
d. Debit spread

41. In finance, a _________ is a standardized contract, to buy or sell a specified commodity of standardized quality at a certain date in the future, at a market determined price (the futures price.)

The price is determined by the instantaneous equilibrium between the forces of supply and demand among competing buy and sell orders on the exchange at the time of the purchase or sale of the contract.

In many cases, the items may be such non-traditional 'commodities' as foreign currencies, commercial or government paper [e.g., bonds], or 'baskets' of corporate equity ['stock indices'] or other financial instruments.

a. Repurchase agreement
b. Heston model
c. Financial future
d. Futures contract

42. In finance, a _________ is a derivative in which two counterparties agree to exchange one stream of cash flows against another stream. These streams are called the legs of the _________.

The cash flows are calculated over a notional principal amount, which is usually not exchanged between counterparties.

a. Volatility swap
b. Volatility arbitrage
c. Local volatility
d. Swap

43. A _________ is an exchange of promises between two or more parties to do an act which is enforceable in a court of law. It is where an unqualified offer meets a qualified acceptance and the parties reach Consensus ad Idem. The parties must have the necessary capacity to _________ and the _________ must not be either trifling, indeterminate, impossible or illegal.

a. 4-4-5 Calendar
b. 529 plan
c. 7-Eleven
d. Contract

44. In finance, _________ (or gearing) is borrowing money to supplement existing funds for investment in such a way that the potential positive or negative outcome is magnified and/or enhanced. It generally refers to using borrowed funds, or debt, so as to attempt to increase the returns to equity. Deleveraging is the action of reducing borrowings.

a. Financial endowment
b. Limited partnership
c. Pension fund
d. Leverage

45. In economics, business, and accounting, a _________ is the value of money that has been used up to produce something, and hence is not available for use anymore. In business, the _________ may be one of acquisition, in which case the amount of money expended to acquire it is counted as _________. In this case, money is the input that is gone in order to acquire the thing.

a. Marginal cost
b. Fixed costs
c. Sliding scale fees
d. Cost

46. _________, is when a company issues common stock or shares to the public for the first time. They are often issued by smaller, younger companies seeking capital to expand, but can also be done by large privately-owned companies looking to become publicly traded.

In an _________ the issuer may obtain the assistance of an underwriting firm, which helps it determine what type of security to issue (common or preferred), best offering price and time to bring it to market.

a. Asian Financial Crisis
b. Interest
c. Insolvency
d. Initial public offering

1. A _________ is a member of an exchange who is an employee of a member firm and executes orders, as agent, on the floor of the exchange for clients. The _________ receives an order via teletype machine from his firm's trading department and then proceeds to the appropriate trading post on the exchange floor. There he joins other brokers and the specialist in the security being bought or sold and executes the trade at the best competitive price available.
   a. Case-Shiller Home Price Indices
   b. Multivariate normal distribution
   c. Business valuation standards
   d. Floor broker

2. In finance, _________ (or gearing) is borrowing money to supplement existing funds for investment in such a way that the potential positive or negative outcome is magnified and/or enhanced. It generally refers to using borrowed funds, or debt, so as to attempt to increase the returns to equity. Deleveraging is the action of reducing borrowings.
   a. Limited partnership
   b. Pension fund
   c. Financial endowment
   d. Leverage

3. In economics, business, and accounting, a _________ is the value of money that has been used up to produce something, and hence is not available for use anymore. In business, the _________ may be one of acquisition, in which case the amount of money expended to acquire it is counted as _________. In this case, money is the input that is gone in order to acquire the thing.
   a. Fixed costs
   b. Cost
   c. Sliding scale fees
   d. Marginal cost

4. In finance, an _________ is the difference between the expected return of a security and the actual return. _________s are sometimes triggered by 'events.' Events can include mergers, dividend announcements, company earning announcements, interest rate increases, lawsuits, etc. all which can contribute to an _________.
   a. AAB
   b. ABN Amro
   c. A Random Walk Down Wall Street
   d. Abnormal return

5. In business and accounting, _________s are everything of value that is owned by a person or company. The balance sheet of a firm records the monetary value of the _________s owned by the firm. The two major _________ classes are tangible _________s and intangible _________s.

a. Accounts payable
b. EBITDA
c. Income
d. Asset

6. In finance, _________ is the process of estimating the potential market value of a financial asset or liability. they can be done on assets (for example, investments in marketable securities such as stocks, options, business enterprises, or intangible assets such as patents and trademarks) or on liabilities (e.g., Bonds issued by a company.) _________s are required in many contexts including investment analysis, capital budgeting, merger and acquisition transactions, financial reporting, taxable events to determine the proper tax liability, and in litigation.
a. Margin
b. Valuation
c. Share
d. Procter ' Gamble

7. In finance, the _________ is the global financial market for short-term borrowing and lending. It provides short-term liquidity funding for the global financial system. The _________ is where short-term obligations such as Treasury bills, commercial paper and bankers' acceptances are bought and sold.
a. Cramdown
b. Debt-for-equity swap
c. Money market
d. Consumer debt

8. _________ is that which is owed; usually referencing assets owed, but the term can cover other obligations. In the case of assets, _________ is a means of using future purchasing power in the present before a summation has been earned. Some companies and corporations use _________ as a part of their overall corporate finance strategy.
a. Cross-collateralization
b. Partial Payment
c. Credit cycle
d. Debt

9. The _________ is the financial market where previously issued securities and financial instruments such as stock, bonds, options, and futures are bought and sold. The term '_________' is also used refer to the market for any used goods or assets, or an alternative use for an existing product or asset where the customer base is the second market

With primary issuances of securities or financial instruments, or the primary market, investors purchase these securities directly from issuers such as corporations issuing shares in an IPO or private placement, or directly from the federal government in the case of treasuries.

a. Delta neutral
b. Secondary market
c. Performance attribution
d. Financial market

10. A _________ is a financial contract whose value is derived from the value of something else (known as the underlying.) The underlying on which a _________ is based can be an asset, weather conditions bonds or other forms of credit.

a. 529 plan
b. Derivative
c. 7-Eleven
d. 4-4-5 Calendar

11. A _________ is a private or public market for the trading of company stock and derivatives of company stock at an agreed price; these are securities listed on a stock exchange as well as those only traded privately.

The size of the world _________ is estimated at about $36.6 trillion US at the beginning of October 2008 . The world derivatives market has been estimated at about $480 trillion face or nominal value, 12 times the size of the entire world economy.

a. Adolph Coors
b. Andrew Tobias
c. Stock market
d. Anton Gelonkin

12. _________, is when a company issues common stock or shares to the public for the first time. They are often issued by smaller, younger companies seeking capital to expand, but can also be done by large privately-owned companies looking to become publicly traded.

In an _________ the issuer may obtain the assistance of an underwriting firm, which helps it determine what type of security to issue (common or preferred), best offering price and time to bring it to market.

a. Interest
b. Insolvency
c. Asian Financial Crisis
d. Initial public offering

13. A _________ is a fungible, negotiable instrument representing financial value. They are broadly categorized into debt securities (such as banknotes, bonds and debentures), and equity securities; e.g., common stocks. The company or other entity issuing the _________ is called the issuer.

a. Securities lending
b. Book entry
c. Tracking stock
d. Security

14. A _________ is the highest price that a buyer (i.e., bidder) is willing to pay for a good. It is usually referred to simply as the 'bid.'

In bid and ask, the _________ stands in contrast to the ask price or 'offer', and the difference between the two is called the bid/ask spread.

An unsolicited bid or offer is when a person or company receives a bid even though they are not looking to sell.

a. Bid price
b. Settlement date
c. Political risk
d. Mid price

15. A _________, securities exchange or (in Europe) bourse is a corporation or mutual organization which provides 'trading' facilities for stock brokers and traders, to trade stocks and other securities. _________s also provide facilities for the issue and redemption of securities as well as other financial instruments and capital events including the payment of income and dividends. The securities traded on a _________ include: shares issued by companies, unit trusts and other pooled investment products and bonds.

a. 4-4-5 Calendar
b. Stock exchange
c. 529 plan
d. 7-Eleven

16. An _________ is the term used in financial circles for a type of computer system that facilitates trading of financial products outside of stock exchanges. The primary products that are traded on an _________ are stocks and currencies. They came into existence in 1998 when the SEC authorized their creation.

a. Insider trading
b. Open outcry
c. Intellidex
d. Electronic communication network

17. A _________ or bank is a financial institution whose primary activity is to act as a payment agent for customers and to borrow and lend money.

The first modern bank was founded in Italy in Genoa in 1406, its name was Banco di San Giorgio (Bank of St. George.)

Many other financial activities were added over time.

a. 4-4-5 Calendar
b. Bought deal
c. Black Sea Trade and Development Bank
d. Banker

18. The U.S. _________ is an independent agency of the United States government which holds primary responsibility for enforcing the federal securities laws and regulating the securities industry, the nation's stock and options exchanges, and other electronic securities markets. The SEC was created by section 4 of the SEC of 1934 (now codified as 15 U.S.C. Â§ 78d and commonly referred to as the 1934 Act.)

a. 529 plan
b. 7-Eleven
c. 4-4-5 Calendar
d. Securities and Exchange Commission

19. _________ is an arrangement with the U.S. Securities and Exchange Commission that allows a single registration document to be filed that permits the issuance of multiple securities.

_________ is a registration of a new issue which can be prepared up to two years in advance, so that the issue can be offered quickly as soon as funds are needed or market conditions are favorable.

For example, current market conditions in the housing market are not favorable for a specific firm to issue a public offering.

a. Black Sea Trade and Development Bank
b. Bought deal
c. 4-4-5 Calendar
d. Shelf registration

1. The institution most often referenced by the word '_________' is a public or publicly traded _________, the shares of which are traded on a public stock exchange (e.g., the New York Stock Exchange or Nasdaq in the United States) where shares of stock of _________s are bought and sold by and to the general public. Most of the largest businesses in the world are publicly traded _________s. However, the majority of _________s are said to be closely held, privately held or close _________s, meaning that no ready market exists for the trading of shares.

a. Corporation
b. Federal Home Loan Mortgage Corporation
c. Protect
d. Depository Trust Company

2. The phrase _________ refers to the aspect of corporate strategy, corporate finance and management dealing with the buying, selling and combining of different companies that can aid, finance, or help a growing company in a given industry grow rapidly without having to create another business entity.

An acquisition, also known as a takeover, is the buying of one company (the 'target') by another. An acquisition may be friendly or hostile.

a. Mergers and acquisitions
b. 4-4-5 Calendar
c. 7-Eleven
d. 529 plan

3. _________ is a diversified financial services company with operations around the world. Wells Fargo is the fourth largest bank in the US by assets and the second largest bank by market cap.

a. Federal Deposit Insurance Corporation
b. Gold exchange-traded fund
c. Wells Fargo ' Co.
d. Holding company

4. _________, in bookkeeping, refers to assets, liabilities, income, and expenses recorded on individual pages of the so called book of final entry or ledger. Changes in _________ value are made by chronologically posting debit (DR) and credit (CR) entries to its page. Examples of _________s are cash, _________s receivable, mortgages, loans, land and buildings, common stock, sales, services provided, wages, and payroll overhead.

a. Alpha
b. Option
c. Accretion
d. Account

5. A _________ is a fungible, negotiable instrument representing financial value. They are broadly categorized into debt securities (such as banknotes, bonds and debentures), and equity securities; e.g., common stocks. The company or other entity issuing the _________ is called the issuer.
   a. Book entry
   b. Tracking stock
   c. Securities lending
   d. Security

6. _________ is a fee paid on borrowed assets. It is the price paid for the use of borrowed money , or, money earned by deposited funds . Assets that are sometimes lent with _________ include money, shares, consumer goods through hire purchase, major assets such as aircraft, and even entire factories in finance lease arrangements.
   a. A Random Walk Down Wall Street
   b. Interest
   c. AAB
   d. Insolvency

7. An _________ is the price a borrower pays for the use of money they do not own, and the return a lender receives for deferring the use of funds, by lending it to the borrower. _________s are normally expressed as a percentage rate over the period of one year.

   _________s targets are also a vital tool of monetary policy and are used to control variables like investment, inflation, and unemployment.

   a. Interest rate
   b. A Random Walk Down Wall Street
   c. ABN Amro
   d. AAB

8. In finance, _________ (or gearing) is borrowing money to supplement existing funds for investment in such a way that the potential positive or negative outcome is magnified and/or enhanced. It generally refers to using borrowed funds, or debt, so as to attempt to increase the returns to equity. Deleveraging is the action of reducing borrowings.
   a. Leverage
   b. Pension fund
   c. Financial endowment
   d. Limited partnership

9.

A _________ is a type of financial intermediary and a type of bank. Commercial banking is also known as business banking. It is a bank that provides checking accounts, savings accounts, and money market accounts and that accepts time deposits.

a. 4-4-5 Calendar
b. 529 plan
c. Commercial bank
d. 7-Eleven

10. _________ is the provision of resources (such as granting a loan) by one party to another party where that second party does not reimburse the first party immediately, thereby generating a debt, and instead arranges either to repay or return those resources (or material(s) of equal value) at a later date. The first party is called a creditor, also known as a lender, while the second party is called a debtor, also known as a borrower.

Movements of financial capital are normally dependent on either _________ or equity transfers.

a. Comparable
b. Credit
c. Warrant
d. Clearing house

11. A _________ is a cooperative financial institution that is owned and controlled by its members, and operated for the purpose of promoting thrift, providing credit at reasonable rates, and providing other financial services to its members. Many _________s exist to further community development or sustainable international development on a local level. Worldwide, _________ systems vary significantly in terms of total system assets and average institution asset size since _________s exist in a wide range of sizes, ranging from volunteer operations with a handful of members to institutions with several billion dollars in assets and hundreds of thousands of members.

a. Credit Union Service Organization
b. Credit union
c. Corporate credit union
d. Fi-linx

12. A _________ is a professionally managed type of collective investment scheme that pools money from many investors and invests it in stocks, bonds, short-term money market instruments, and/or other securities. The _________ will have a fund manager that trades the pooled money on a regular basis. Currently, the worldwide value of all _________s totals more than $26 trillion.

Since 1940, there have been three basic types of investment companies in the United States: open-end funds, also known in the US as _________s; unit investment trusts (UITs); and closed-end funds.

a. Trust company
b. Net asset value
c. Financial intermediary
d. Mutual fund

13. _________ is a life insurance policy that remains in force for the insured's whole life and requires (in most cases) premiums to be paid every year into the policy.

All life insurance was originally term insurance. However, because term life insurance only pays a claim upon death within the stated term, most term insurance policy holders became upset over the idea that they could be paying premiums for 20 or 30 years and then wind up with nothing to show for it.

a. Whole life insurance
b. Term life insurance
c. 529 plan
d. 4-4-5 Calendar

14. In financial accounting, the term _________ is most commonly used to describe any part of shareholders' equity, except for basic share capital. Sometimes, the term is used instead of the term provision; such a use, however, is inconsistent with the terminology suggested by International Accounting Standards Board. For more information about provisions, see provision (accounting.)

a. FIFO and LIFO accounting
b. Treasury stock
c. Closing entries
d. Reserve

15. A _________ is a pool of assets forming an independent legal entity that are bought with the contributions to a pension plan for the exclusive purpose of financing pension plan benefits.

_________s are important shareholders of listed and private companies. They are especially important to the stock market where large institutional investors like the Ontario Teachers' Pension Plan dominate.

a. Leverage
b. Limited liability company
c. Leveraged buyout
d. Pension fund

16. Explicit _________ is a measure implemented in many countries to protect bank depositors, in full or in part, from losses caused by a bank's inability to pay its debts when due. _________ systems are one component of a financial system safety net that promotes financial stability.

a. Time deposit
b. Deposit Insurance
c. Reserve requirement
d. Banking panic

17. The _________ is a United States government corporation created by the Glass-Steagall Act of 1933. It provides deposit insurance, which guarantees the safety of checking and savings deposits in member banks, currently up to $250,000 per depositor per bank. Insured deposits are backed by the full faith and credit of the United States.

a. Federal Deposit Insurance Corporation
b. FASB
c. NYSE Group
d. Ford Foundation

18. In business and finance, a _________ (also referred to as equity _________) of stock means a _________ of ownership in a corporation (company.) In the plural, stocks is often used as a synonym for _________s especially in the United States, but it is less commonly used that way outside of North America.

In the United Kingdom, South Africa, and Australia, stock can also refer to completely different financial instruments such as government bonds or, less commonly, to all kinds of marketable securities.

a. Procter ' Gamble
b. Bucket shop
c. Margin
d. Share

19. The _________ of 1974 (Pub.L. 93-406, 88 Stat. 829, enacted September 2, 1974) is an American federal statute that establishes minimum standards for pension plans in private industry and provides for extensive rules on the federal income tax effects of transactions associated with employee benefit plans.

a. Express warranty
b. Expedited Funds Availability Act
c. Articles of Partnership
d. Employee Retirement Income Security Act

20. _________, refers to consumption opportunity gained by an entity within a specified time frame, which is generally expressed in monetary terms. However, for households and individuals, '_________ is the sum of all the wages, salaries, profits, interests payments, rents and other forms of earnings received... in a given period of time.' For firms, _________ generally refers to net-profit: what remains of revenue after expenses have been subtracted.

a. Annual report
b. Accrual
c. OIBDA
d. Income

21. An _________ is a company whose main business is holding securities of other companies purely for investment purposes. The _________ invests money on behalf of its shareholders who in turn share in the profits and losses.

a. A Random Walk Down Wall Street
b. AAB
c. Unit investment trust
d. Investment Company

22. The _________, an agency of the United States Department of the Treasury, is the primary regulator of federal savings associations (sometimes referred to as federal thrifts.) Federal savings associations include both federal savings banks and federal savings and loans. The OTS is also responsible for supervising savings and loan holding companies (SLHCs) and some state-chartered institutions.

a. AAB
b. A Random Walk Down Wall Street
c. ABN Amro
d. Office of Thrift Supervision

23. The U.S. _________ is an independent agency of the United States government which holds primary responsibility for enforcing the federal securities laws and regulating the securities industry, the nation's stock and options exchanges, and other electronic securities markets. The SEC was created by section 4 of the SEC of 1934 (now codified as 15 U.S.C. Â§ 78d and commonly referred to as the 1934 Act.)

a. 4-4-5 Calendar
b. 7-Eleven
c. 529 plan
d. Securities and Exchange Commission

24. A _________ is a company that owns other companies' outstanding stock. It usually refers to a company which does not produce goods or services itself, rather its only purpose is owning shares of other companies. They allow the reduction of risk for the owners and can allow the ownership and control of a number of different companies.

a. Privately held company
b. MRU Holdings
c. Federal National Mortgage Association
d. Holding company

25. _________ is the process by which the government, or monetary authority of a country controls (i) the supply of money central bank (ii) availability of money, and (iii) cost of money or rate of interest, in order to attain a set of objectives oriented towards the growth and stability of the economy. Monetary theory provides insight into how to craft optimal _________.

_________ is referred to as either being an expansionary policy where an expansionary policy increases the total supply of money in the economy, and a contractionary policy decreases the total money supply.

a. Tax exemption
b. Federal Open Market Committee
c. Natural resources consumption tax
d. Monetary policy

26. _________ are the means of implementing monetary policy by which a central bank controls its national money supply by buying and selling government securities, or other financial instruments. Monetary targets, such as interest rates or exchange rates, are used to guide this implementation.

Since most money is now in the form of electronic records, rather than paper records such as banknotes, _________ are conducted simply by electronically increasing or decreasing ('crediting' or 'debiting') the amount of money that a bank has, e.g., in its reserve account at the central bank, in exchange for a bank selling or buying a financial instrument.

a. AAB
b. Open market operations
c. ABN Amro
d. A Random Walk Down Wall Street

27. The _________ is a bank regulation that sets the minimum reserves each bank must hold to customer deposits and notes. These reserves are designed to satisfy withdrawal demands, and would normally be in the form of fiat currency stored in a bank vault (vault cash), or with a central bank.

The reserve ratio is sometimes used as a tool in the monetary policy, influencing the country's economy, borrowing, and interest rates.

a. Prime rate
b. Wall Street Journal prime rate
c. Variable rate mortgage
d. Reserve requirement

28. _________ is the removal or simplification of government rules and regulations that constrain the operation of market forces. _________ does not mean elimination of laws against fraud, but eliminating or reducing government control of how business is done, thereby moving toward a more free market.

The stated rationale for '_________' is often that fewer and simpler regulations will lead to a raised level of competitiveness, therefore higher productivity, more efficiency and lower prices overall.

a. Demand shock
b. Supply shock
c. Deregulation
d. Value added

29. A '_________' is a 'Charge' that is paid to obtain the right to delay a payment. Essentially, the payer purchases the right to make a given payment in the future instead of in the Present. The '_________', or 'Charge' that must be paid to delay the payment, is simply the difference between what the payment amount would be if it were paid in the present and what the payment amount would be paid if it were paid in the future.
a. Risk aversion
b. Value at risk
c. Discount
d. Risk modeling

30. The _________ is an interest rate a central bank charges depository institutions that borrow reserves from it.

The term _________ has two meanings:

- the same as interest rate; the term 'discount' does not refer to the meaning of the word, but to the purpose of using the quantity, such as computations of present value, e.g. net present value / discounted cash flow

- the annual effective _________, which is the annual interest divided by the capital including that interest; this rate is lower than the interest rate; it corresponds to using the value after a year as the nominal value, and seeing the initial value as the nominal value minus a discount; it is used for Treasury Bills and similar financial instruments

The annual effective _________ is the annual interest divided by the capital including that interest, which is the interest rate divided by 100% plus the interest rate. It is the annual discount factor to be applied to the future cash flow, to find the discount, subtracted from a future value to find the value one year earlier.

For example, suppose there is a government bond that sells for $95 and pays $100 in a year's time.

a. Discount rate
b. Black-Scholes
c. Fisher equation
d. Stochastic volatility

31. The _________ Act is an Act of the 106th United States Congress which repealed part of the Glass-Steagall Act of 1933, opening up competition among banks, securities companies and insurance companies. The Glass-Steagall Act prohibited any one institution from acting as both an investment bank and a commercial bank, or as both a bank and an insurer.

The _________ Act (GLBA) allowed commercial and investment banks to consolidate.

a. 7-Eleven
b. 529 plan
c. Gramm-Leach-Bliley
d. 4-4-5 Calendar

32. A _________ or bank is a financial institution whose primary activity is to act as a payment agent for customers and to borrow and lend money.

The first modern bank was founded in Italy in Genoa in 1406, its name was Banco di San Giorgio (Bank of St. George.)

Many other financial activities were added over time.

a. Bought deal
b. Banker
c. 4-4-5 Calendar
d. Black Sea Trade and Development Bank

1. _________ is a fee paid on borrowed assets. It is the price paid for the use of borrowed money , or, money earned by deposited funds . Assets that are sometimes lent with _________ include money, shares, consumer goods through hire purchase, major assets such as aircraft, and even entire factories in finance lease arrangements.

a. Insolvency
b. A Random Walk Down Wall Street
c. Interest
d. AAB

2. The phrase _________ refers to the aspect of corporate strategy, corporate finance and management dealing with the buying, selling and combining of different companies that can aid, finance, or help a growing company in a given industry grow rapidly without having to create another business entity.

An acquisition, also known as a takeover, is the buying of one company (the 'target') by another. An acquisition may be friendly or hostile.

a. Mergers and acquisitions
b. 7-Eleven
c. 4-4-5 Calendar
d. 529 plan

3. _________ mature in one year or less. Like zero-coupon bonds, they do not pay interest prior to maturity; instead they are sold at a discount of the par value to create a positive yield to maturity. Many regard _________ as the least risky investment available to U.S. investors.

a. 4-4-5 Calendar
b. Treasury Inflation Protected Securities
c. Treasury securities
d. Treasury bills

4. In finance, a _________ is a debt security, in which the authorized issuer owes the holders a debt and, depending on the terms of the _________, is obliged to pay interest (the coupon) and/or to repay the principal at a later date, termed maturity.

Thus a _________ is a loan: the issuer is the borrower, the _________ holder is the lender, and the coupon is the interest. _________s provide the borrower with external funds to finance long-term investments, or, in the case of government _________s, to finance current expenditure.

a. Catastrophe bonds
b. Convertible bond
c. Puttable bond
d. Bond

5. An _________ is the price a borrower pays for the use of money they do not own, and the return a lender receives for deferring the use of funds, by lending it to the borrower. _________s are normally expressed as a percentage rate over the period of one year.

_________s targets are also a vital tool of monetary policy and are used to control variables like investment, inflation, and unemployment.

a. A Random Walk Down Wall Street
b. ABN Amro
c. AAB
d. Interest rate

6. In business and finance, a _________ (also referred to as equity _________) of stock means a _________ of ownership in a corporation (company.) In the plural, stocks is often used as a synonym for _________s especially in the United States, but it is less commonly used that way outside of North America.

In the United Kingdom, South Africa, and Australia, stock can also refer to completely different financial instruments such as government bonds or, less commonly, to all kinds of marketable securities.

a. Bucket shop
b. Margin
c. Procter ' Gamble
d. Share

7. In finance, the term _________ describes the amount in cash that returns to the owners of a security. Normally it does not include the price variations, at the difference of the total return. _________ applies to various stated rates of return on stocks (common and preferred, and convertible), fixed income instruments (bonds, notes, bills, strips, zero coupon), and some other investment type insurance products (e.g. annuities.)
a. Macaulay duration
b. 4-4-5 Calendar
c. Yield to maturity
d. Yield

8. _________ is that which is owed; usually referencing assets owed, but the term can cover other obligations. In the case of assets, _________ is a means of using future purchasing power in the present before a summation has been earned. Some companies and corporations use _________ as a part of their overall corporate finance strategy.

a. Cross-collateralization
b. Debt
c. Partial Payment
d. Credit cycle

9. In economics, _________ is a rise in the general level of prices of goods and services in an economy over a period of time. The term '_________' once referred to increases in the money supply (monetary _________); however, economic debates about the relationship between money supply and price levels have led to its primary use today in describing price _________. _________ can also be described as a decline in the real value of money--a loss of purchasing power in the medium of exchange which is also the monetary unit of account.

a. AAB
b. A Random Walk Down Wall Street
c. ABN Amro
d. Inflation

10. The _________ is the market for securities, where companies and governments can raise longterm funds. The _________ includes the stock market and the bond market. Financial regulators, such as the U.S. Securities and Exchange Commission, oversee the _________s in their designated countries to ensure that investors are protected against fraud.

a. Delta neutral
b. Forward market
c. Capital market
d. Spot rate

11. A _________ is the price of a single share of a no. of saleable stocks of the company. Once the stock is purchased, the owner becomes a shareholder of the company that issued the share.

a. Whisper numbers
b. Stock split
c. Share price
d. Trading curb

12. In finance, _________ (or gearing) is borrowing money to supplement existing funds for investment in such a way that the potential positive or negative outcome is magnified and/or enhanced. It generally refers to using borrowed funds, or debt, so as to attempt to increase the returns to equity. Deleveraging is the action of reducing borrowings.

a. Limited partnership
b. Pension fund
c. Financial endowment
d. Leverage

13. In economic models, the _________ time frame assumes no fixed factors of production. Firms can enter or leave the marketplace, and the cost (and availability) of land, labor, raw materials, and capital goods can be assumed to vary. In contrast, in the short-run time frame, certain factors are assumed to be fixed, because there is not sufficient time for them to change.
a. Short-run
b. 529 plan
c. 4-4-5 Calendar
d. Long-run

14. In economics, the concept of the _________ refers to the decision-making time frame of a firm in which at least one factor of production is fixed. Costs which are fixed in the _________ have no impact on a firms decisions. For example a firm can raise output by increasing the amount of labour through overtime.
a. 529 plan
b. Long-run
c. 4-4-5 Calendar
d. Short-run

15. A _________ is a fungible, negotiable instrument representing financial value. They are broadly categorized into debt securities (such as banknotes, bonds and debentures), and equity securities; e.g., common stocks. The company or other entity issuing the _________ is called the issuer.
a. Security
b. Tracking stock
c. Book entry
d. Securities lending

16. A _________ is a property interest created by agreement or by operation of law over assets to secure the performance of an obligation, usually the payment of a debt. It gives the beneficiary of the _________ certain preferential rights in the disposition of secured assets. Such rights vary according to the type of _________, but in most cases, a holder of the _________ is entitled to seize, and usually sell, the property to discharge the debt that the _________ secures.

a. FIDC
b. Netting
c. Retention ratio
d. Security Interest

17. In finance, _________ occurs when a debtor has not met its legal obligations according to the debt contract, e.g. it has not made a scheduled payment, or has violated a loan covenant (condition) of the debt contract. _________ may occur if the debtor is either unwilling or unable to pay their debt. This can occur with all debt obligations including bonds, mortgages, loans, and promissory notes.
a. Debt validation
b. Credit crunch
c. Vendor finance
d. Default

18. _________ is the risk of loss due to a debtor's non-payment of a loan or other line of credit (either the principal or interest (coupon) or both)

Most lenders employ their own models (credit scorecards) to rank potential and existing customers according to risk, and then apply appropriate strategies. With products such as unsecured personal loans or mortgages, lenders charge a higher price for higher risk customers and vice versa. With revolving products such as credit cards and overdrafts, risk is controlled through careful setting of credit limits.

a. Liquidity risk
b. Transaction risk
c. Credit risk
d. Market risk

19.

In finance, the _________ can be the expected rate of return above the risk-free interest rate. When measuring risk, a common sense approach is to compare the risk-free return on T-bills and the very risky return on other investments. The difference between these two returns can be interpreted as a measure of the excess return on the average risky asset. This excess return is known as the _________.

a. Risk aversion
b. Risk premium
c. Risk adjusted return on capital
d. Risk modeling

20. _________ is a measure of the ability of a debtor to pay their debts as and when they fall due. It is usually expressed as a ratio or a percentage of current liabilities.

For a corporation with a published balance sheet there are various ratios used to calculate a measure of liquidity.

a. Operating leverage
b. Operating profit margin
c. Invested capital
d. Accounting liquidity

21. _________ is a term used to explain a difference between two types of financial securities (e.g. stocks), that have all the same qualities except liquidity. For example:

_________ is a segment of a three-part theory that works to explain the behavior of yield curves for interest rates. The upwards-curving component of the interest yield can be explained by the _________.

a. 7-Eleven
b. 4-4-5 Calendar
c. 529 plan
d. Liquidity premium

22. _________ is a life of security. It may also refer to the final payment date of a loan or other financial instrument, at which point all remaining interest and principal is due to be paid.

1, 3, 6 months _________ band can be calculated by using 30-day per month periods.

a. False billing
b. Maturity
c. Replacement cost
d. Primary market

23. John Maynard Keynes developed the _________ of Interest in the General Theory of Employment Interest and Money. The primary consideration of the _________ is the demand for money as an asset, as a means for holding wealth. Interest rates, he argues, cannot be a reward for savings as such because, if a person hoards his savings in cash, keeping it under his mattress say, he will receive no interest, although he has nevertheless, refrained from consuming all his current income.
a. 4-4-5 Calendar
b. 529 plan
c. 7-Eleven
d. Liquidity preference

24. _________ are government bonds issued by the United States Department of the Treasury through the Bureau of the Public Debt. They are the debt financing instruments of the U.S. Federal government, and they are often referred to simply as Treasuries or Treasurys. There are four types of marketable _________: Treasury bills, Treasury notes, Treasury bonds, and Treasury Inflation Protected Securities (TIPS.)
a. Treasury Inflation-Protected Securities
b. Treasury securities
c. Treasury Inflation Protected Securities
d. 4-4-5 Calendar

25. In finance, the _________ is the relation between the interest rate (or cost of borrowing) and the time to maturity of the debt for a given borrower in a given currency. For example, the current U.S. dollar interest rates paid on U.S. Treasury securities for various maturities are closely watched by many traders, and are commonly plotted on a graph such as the one on the right which is informally called 'the _________.' More formal mathematical descriptions of this relation are often called the term structure of interest rates.

The yield of a debt instrument is the annualized percentage increase in the value of the investment.

a. 529 plan
b. 4-4-5 Calendar
c. 7-Eleven
d. Yield curve

26. In financial accounting, the term _________ is most commonly used to describe any part of shareholders' equity, except for basic share capital. Sometimes, the term is used instead of the term provision; such a use, however, is inconsistent with the terminology suggested by International Accounting Standards Board. For more information about provisions, see provision (accounting.)

a. Closing entries
b. FIFO and LIFO accounting
c. Treasury stock
d. Reserve

27. In business and accounting, _________s are everything of value that is owned by a person or company. The balance sheet of a firm records the monetary value of the _________s owned by the firm. The two major _________ classes are tangible _________s and intangible _________s.
a. Income
b. Asset
c. EBITDA
d. Accounts payable

28. In finance, _________ is the process of estimating the potential market value of a financial asset or liability. they can be done on assets (for example, investments in marketable securities such as stocks, options, business enterprises, or intangible assets such as patents and trademarks) or on liabilities (e.g., Bonds issued by a company.) _________s are required in many contexts including investment analysis, capital budgeting, merger and acquisition transactions, financial reporting, taxable events to determine the proper tax liability, and in litigation.
a. Procter ' Gamble
b. Share
c. Margin
d. Valuation

29. A _________ is a payment made by a corporation to its shareholder members. When a corporation earns a profit or surplus, that money can be put to two uses: it can either be re-invested in the business (called retained earnings), or it can be paid to the shareholders as a _________. Many corporations retain a portion of their earnings and pay the remainder as a _________.
a. Dividend puzzle
b. Special dividend
c. Dividend yield
d. Dividend

1. The institution most often referenced by the word '_________' is a public or publicly traded _________, the shares of which are traded on a public stock exchange (e.g., the New York Stock Exchange or Nasdaq in the United States) where shares of stock of _________s are bought and sold by and to the general public. Most of the largest businesses in the world are publicly traded _________s. However, the majority of _________s are said to be closely held, privately held or close _________s, meaning that no ready market exists for the trading of shares.

a. Depository Trust Company
b. Protect
c. Federal Home Loan Mortgage Corporation
d. Corporation

2. A mutual shareholder or _________ is an individual or company (including a corporation) that legally owns one or more shares of stock in a joint stock company. A company's shareholders collectively own that company. Thus, the typical goal of such companies is to enhance shareholder value.

a. Stock market bubble
b. Limit order
c. Trading curb
d. Stockholder

3. In business and accounting, _________s are everything of value that is owned by a person or company. The balance sheet of a firm records the monetary value of the _________s owned by the firm. The two major _________ classes are tangible _________s and intangible _________s.

a. Accounts payable
b. Income
c. EBITDA
d. Asset

4. _________ is the balance of the amounts of cash being received and paid by a business during a defined period of time, sometimes tied to a specific project. Measurement of _________ can be used

- to evaluate the state or performance of a business or project.
- to determine problems with liquidity. Being profitable does not necessarily mean being liquid. A company can fail because of a shortage of cash, even while profitable.
- to generate project rate of returns. The time of _________s into and out of projects are used as inputs to financial models such as internal rate of return, and net present value.
- to examine income or growth of a business when it is believed that accrual accounting concepts do not represent economic realities. Alternately, _________ can be used to 'validate' the net income generated by accrual accounting.

_________ as a generic term may be used differently depending on context, and certain _________ definitions may be adapted by analysts and users for their own uses. Common terms include operating _________ and free _________.

_________s can be classified into:

1. Operational _________s: Cash received or expended as a result of the company's core business activities.
2. Investment _________s: Cash received or expended through capital expenditure, investments or acquisitions.
3. Financing _________s: Cash received or expended as a result of financial activities, such as interests and dividends.

All three together - the net _________ - are necessary to reconcile the beginning cash balance to the ending cash balance. Loan draw downs or equity injections, that is just shifting of capital but no expenditure as such, are not considered in the net _________.

a. Shareholder value
b. Real option
c. Cash flow
d. Corporate finance

5. In accounting, a _________ is an asset on the balance sheet which is expected to be sold or otherwise used up in the near future, usually within one year, or one business cycle - whichever is longer. Typical _________s include cash, cash equivalents, accounts receivable, inventory, the portion of prepaid accounts which will be used within a year, and short-term investments.

On the balance sheet, assets will typically be classified into _________s and long-term assets.

a. Long-term liabilities
b. Write-off
c. Historical cost
d. Current asset

6. _________ is a fee paid on borrowed assets. It is the price paid for the use of borrowed money , or, money earned by deposited funds . Assets that are sometimes lent with _________ include money, shares, consumer goods through hire purchase, major assets such as aircraft, and even entire factories in finance lease arrangements.
a. Interest
b. Insolvency
c. AAB
d. A Random Walk Down Wall Street

7. A _________ is a type of business entity in which partners (owners) share with each other the profits or losses of the business undertaking in which all have invested. _________s are often favored over corporations for taxation purposes, as the _________ structure does not generally incur a tax on profits before it is distributed to the partners (i.e. there is no dividend tax levied.) However, depending on the _________ structure and the jurisdiction in which it operates, owners of a _________ may be exposed to greater personal liability than they would as shareholders of a corporation.

a. Fiduciary
b. National Securities Markets Improvement Act of 1996
c. Clayton Antitrust Act
d. Partnership

8. A sole _________, or simply _________ is a type of business entity which legally has no separate existence from its owner. Hence, the limitations of liability enjoyed by a corporation and limited liability partnerships do not apply to sole proprietors. All debts of the business are debts of the owner.

a. Just-in-time
b. Proprietorship
c. Product life cycle
d. Free cash flow

9. A _________ is a form of partnership similar to a general partnership, except that in addition to one or more general partners (GPs), there are one or more limited partners (_________s). It is a partnership in which only one partner is required to be a general partner.

The GPs are, in all major respects, in the same legal position as partners in a conventional firm, i.e. they have management control, share the right to use partnership property, share the profits of the firm in predefined proportions, and have joint and several liability for the debts of the partnership.

a. Leverage
b. Limited liability company
c. Fund of funds
d. Limited partnership

10. In finance, _________ are stocks that appreciate in value and yield a high return on equity (ROE.) Analysts compute ROE by taking the company's net income and dividing it by the company's equity. To be classified as a growth stock, analysts expect to see at least 15 percent return on equity.

a. Stock valuation
b. Security Analysis
c. 4-4-5 Calendar
d. Growth stocks

11. In finance, _________, also known as return on investment is the ratio of money gained or lost on an investment relative to the amount of money invested. The amount of money gained or lost may be referred to as interest, profit/loss, gain/loss, or net income/loss. The money invested may be referred to as the asset, capital, principal, or the cost basis of the investment.

a. Doctrine of the Proper Law
b. Stock or scrip dividends
c. Composiition of Creditors
d. Rate of return

12. In finance, _________ is the process of estimating the potential market value of a financial asset or liability. they can be done on assets (for example, investments in marketable securities such as stocks, options, business enterprises, or intangible assets such as patents and trademarks) or on liabilities (e.g., Bonds issued by a company.) _________s are required in many contexts including investment analysis, capital budgeting, merger and acquisition transactions, financial reporting, taxable events to determine the proper tax liability, and in litigation.

a. Procter ' Gamble
b. Margin
c. Valuation
d. Share

13. _________ and the related Fisher's linear discriminant are methods used in statistics and machine learning to find the linear combination of features which best separate two or more classes of objects or events. The resulting combination may be used as a linear classifier, or, more commonly, for dimensionality reduction before later classification.

_________ is closely related to ANOVA (analysis of variance) and regression analysis, which also attempt to express one dependent variable as a linear combination of other features or measurements.

a. 7-Eleven
b. 4-4-5 Calendar
c. 529 plan
d. Linear discriminant analysis

14. _________ are the earnings returned on the initial investment amount.

In the US, the Financial Accounting Standards Board (FASB) requires companies' income statements to report _________ for each of the major categories of the income statement: continuing operations, discontinued operations, extraordinary items, and net income.

The _________ formula does not include preferred dividends for categories outside of continued operations and net income.

a. Inventory turnover
b. Assets turnover
c. Average accounting return
d. Earnings per share

15. _________ is the difference between price and the costs of bringing to market whatever it is that is accounted as an enterprise (whether by harvest, extraction, manufacture, or purchase) in terms of the component costs of delivered goods and/or services and any operating or other expenses.

A key difficulty in measuring profit is in defining costs. Pure economic monetary profits can be zero or negative even in competitive equilibrium when accounted monetized costs exceed monetized price.

a. A Random Walk Down Wall Street
b. Economic profit
c. AAB
d. Accounting profit

16. In economics, _________ is the process by which a firm determines the price and output level that returns the greatest profit. There are several approaches to this problem. The total revenue--total cost method relies on the fact that profit equals revenue minus cost, and the marginal revenue--marginal cost method is based on the fact that total profit in a perfectly competitive market reaches its maximum point where marginal revenue equals marginal cost.
a. Profit maximization
b. Profit margin
c. 4-4-5 Calendar
d. Net profit margin

17. In business and finance, a _________ (also referred to as equity _________) of stock means a _________ of ownership in a corporation (company.) In the plural, stocks is often used as a synonym for _________s especially in the United States, but it is less commonly used that way outside of North America.

In the United Kingdom, South Africa, and Australia, stock can also refer to completely different financial instruments such as government bonds or, less commonly, to all kinds of marketable securities.

a. Procter ' Gamble
b. Margin
c. Bucket shop
d. Share

18. An _________ is a contract written by a seller that conveys to the buyer the right -- but not the obligation -- to buy (in the case of a call _________) or to sell (in the case of a put _________) a particular asset, such as a piece of property such as, among others, a futures contract. In return for granting the _________, the seller collects a payment (the premium) from the buyer.

For example, buying a call _________ provides the right to buy a specified quantity of a security at a set strike price at some time on or before expiration, while buying a put _________ provides the right to sell.

a. Amortization
b. AT'T Mobility LLC
c. Annuity
d. Option

19. An _________ is any government regulation or law that encourages or discourages foreign investment in the local economy, e.g. currency exchange limits.

As globalization integrates the economies of neighboring and of trading states, they are typically forced to trade off such rules as part of a common tax, tariff and trade regime, e.g. as defined by a free trade pact. _________ favoring local investors over global ones is typically discouraged in such pacts, and the idea of a separate _________ rapidly becomes a fiction or fantasy, as real decisions reflect the real need for nations to compete for investment, even from their own local investors.

a. Investment policy
b. A Random Walk Down Wall Street
c. ABN Amro
d. AAB

20. A _________ is a party (e.g. person, organization, company, or government) that has a claim to the services of a second party. The first party, in general, has provided some property or service to the second party under the assumption (usually enforced by contract) that the second party will return an equivalent property or service. The second party is frequently called a debtor or borrower.

a. Creditor
b. False billing
c. Redemption value
d. NOPLAT

21. In business, a _________ is the purchase of one company (the target) by another (the acquirer or bidder). In the UK the term refers to the acquisition of a public company whose shares are listed on a stock exchange, in contrast to the acquisition of a private company.

Before a bidder makes an offer for another company, it usually first informs that company's board of directors.

a. Stock swap
b. 529 plan
c. 4-4-5 Calendar
d. Takeover

22. In finance, the value of an option consists of two components, its intrinsic value and its _________. Time value is simply the difference between option value and intrinsic value. _________ is also known as theta, extrinsic value, or instrumental value.

a. Time value
b. Conservatism
c. Global Squeeze
d. Debt buyer

23. Simply put, _________ is the value of money figuring in a given amount of interest for a given amount of time. For example 100 dollars of todays money held for a year at 5 percent interest is worth 105 dollars, therefore 100 dollars paid now or 105 dollars paid exactly one year from now is the same amount of payment of money with that given intersest at that given amount of time. This notion dates at least to Martín de Azpilcueta of the School of Salamanca.

All of the standard calculations for _________ derive from the most basic algebraic expression for the present value of a future sum, 'discounted' to the present by an amount equal to the _________. For example, a sum of FV to be received in one year is discounted (at the rate of interest r) to give a sum of PV at present: PV = FV -- rÂ·PV = FV/(1+r).

a. Time value of money
b. Coefficient of variation
c. Zero-coupon bond
d. Current account

24. A _________ is a type of limited company in the United Kingdom and the Republic of Ireland which is permitted to offer its shares to the public.

a. 4-4-5 Calendar
b. 7-Eleven
c. Public limited company
d. 529 plan

25. _________, refers to consumption opportunity gained by an entity within a specified time frame, which is generally expressed in monetary terms. However, for households and individuals, '_________ is the sum of all the wages, salaries, profits, interests payments, rents and other forms of earnings received... in a given period of time.' For firms, _________ generally refers to net-profit: what remains of revenue after expenses have been subtracted.

a. Income
b. OIBDA
c. Annual report
d. Accrual

26. An _________ is a tax levied on the financial income of people, corporations, or other legal entities. Various _________ systems exist, with varying degrees of tax incidence. Income taxation can be progressive, proportional, or regressive.

a. A Random Walk Down Wall Street
b. ABN Amro
c. AAB
d. Income tax

27. _________ is the portion of income that is the subject of taxation according to the laws that determine what is income and the taxation rate for that income. Generally, _________ refers to an individual's (or corporation's) gross income, adjusted for various deductions allowable by statute. The main questions put by most individuals in any jurisdiction are 'what makes up my _________' and what tax rates should be applied such that I can work out my tax liability to the state.

a. 529 plan
b. Taxable income
c. 4-4-5 Calendar
d. 7-Eleven

28. A _________ is a profit that results from investments into a capital asset, such as stocks, bonds or real estate, which exceeds the purchase price. It is the difference between a higher selling price and a lower purchase price, resulting in a financial gain for the seller. Conversely, a capital loss arises if the proceeds from the sale of a capital asset are less than the purchase price.

a. Capital gain
b. Tax brackets
c. Payroll tax
d. Capital gains tax

29. A _________ is a payment made by a corporation to its shareholder members. When a corporation earns a profit or surplus, that money can be put to two uses: it can either be re-invested in the business (called retained earnings), or it can be paid to the shareholders as a _________. Many corporations retain a portion of their earnings and pay the remainder as a _________.

a. Dividend yield
b. Special dividend
c. Dividend puzzle
d. Dividend

30. Under the United States Internal Revenue Code, the type of income is defined by its character. _________ is usually characterized as income other than capital gain. _________ can consist of income from wages, salaries, tips, commissions, bonuses, and other types of compensation from employment, interest, dividends, or net income from a sole proprietorship, partnership or LLC.

a. AAB
b. ABN Amro
c. A Random Walk Down Wall Street
d. Ordinary income

31. _________ refers to a tax levied by various jurisdictions on the profits made by companies or associations. It is a tax on the value of the corporation's profits.

The measure of taxable profits varies from country to country.

a. Corporate tax
b. Proxy fight
c. Trade finance
d. First-mover advantage

32. _________ is a term used in accounting, economics and finance to spread the cost of an asset over the span of several years.

In simple words we can say that _________ is the reduction in the value of an asset due to usage, passage of time, wear and tear, technological outdating or obsolescence, depletion or other such factors.

In accounting, _________ is a term used to describe any method of attributing the historical or purchase cost of an asset across its useful life, roughly corresponding to normal wear and tear.

a. Matching principle
b. Deferred financing costs
c. Bottom line
d. Depreciation

33. An _________ is a corporation that makes a valid election to be taxed under Subchapter S of Chapter 1 of the Internal Revenue Code.

In general, _________s do not pay any income taxes. Instead, the corporation's income or losses are divided among and passed through to its shareholders.

a. 7-Eleven
b. 4-4-5 Calendar
c. 529 plan
d. S corporation

34. _________ is one of the largest professional services firms in the world. _________ employs over 123,000 people in a global network of member firms spanning over 145 countries. Composite revenues of _________ member firms in 2007 were $19.8 billion USD (17.4% growth from 2006.)

a. Federal Deposit Insurance Corporation
b. KPMG
c. National Association of State Boards of Accountancy
d. Texas ratio

1. The role of the _________ is to issue accounting standards in the United Kingdom. It is recognised for that purpose under the Companies Act 1985. It took over the task of setting accounting standards from the Accounting Standards Committee (ASC) in 1990.

a. A Random Walk Down Wall Street
b. ABN Amro
c. AAB
d. Accounting Standards Board

2. _________ is the statutory title of qualified accountants in the United States who have passed the Uniform _________ Examination and have met additional state education and experience requirements for certification as a _________. In most U.S. states, only _________s who are licensed are able to provide to the public attestation (including auditing) opinions on financial statements. The exceptions to this rule are Arizona, Kansas, North Carolina and Ohio where, although the '_________' designation is restricted, the practice of auditing is not.

a. Chartered Accountant
b. Certified Public Accountant
c. Chartered Certified Accountant
d. Certified General Accountant

3. _________ is the field of accountancy concerned with the preparation of financial statements for decision makers, such as stockholders, suppliers, banks, employees, government agencies, owners, and other stakeholders. The fundamental need for _________ is to reduce principal-agent problem by measuring and monitoring agents' performance and reporting the results to interested users.

_________ is used to prepare accounting information for people outside the organization or not involved in the day to day running of the company.

a. 529 plan
b. Financial Accounting
c. 7-Eleven
d. 4-4-5 Calendar

4. The _________ is a private, not-for-profit organization whose primary purpose is to develop generally accepted accounting principles (GAAP) within the United States in the public's interest. The Securities and Exchange Commission (SEC) designated the _________ as the organization responsible for setting accounting standards for public companies in the U.S. It was created in 1973, replacing the Accounting Principles Board and the Committee on Accounting Procedure of the American Institute of Certified Public Accountants. The _________'s mission is 'to establish and improve standards of financial accounting and reporting for the guidance and education of the public, including issuers, auditors, and users of financial information.'

The _________ is not a governmental body.

a. Financial Accounting Standards Board
b. World Congress of Accountants
c. KPMG
d. Federal Deposit Insurance Corporation

5. A _________ is a fungible, negotiable instrument representing financial value. They are broadly categorized into debt securities (such as banknotes, bonds and debentures), and equity securities; e.g., common stocks. The company or other entity issuing the _________ is called the issuer.
a. Securities lending
b. Tracking stock
c. Book entry
d. Security

6. The U.S. _________ is an independent agency of the United States government which holds primary responsibility for enforcing the federal securities laws and regulating the securities industry, the nation's stock and options exchanges, and other electronic securities markets. The SEC was created by section 4 of the SEC of 1934 (now codified as 15 U.S.C. Â§ 78d and commonly referred to as the 1934 Act.)
a. 7-Eleven
b. Securities and Exchange Commission
c. 529 plan
d. 4-4-5 Calendar

7. In financial accounting, a _________ or statement of financial position is a summary of a person's or organization's balances. Assets, liabilities and ownership equity are listed as of a specific date, such as the end of its financial year. A _________ is often described as a snapshot of a company's financial condition.
a. Statement on Auditing Standards No. 70: Service Organizations
b. Statement of retained earnings
c. Financial statements
d. Balance sheet

8. _________ is the balance of the amounts of cash being received and paid by a business during a defined period of time, sometimes tied to a specific project. Measurement of _________ can be used

- to evaluate the state or performance of a business or project.
- to determine problems with liquidity. Being profitable does not necessarily mean being liquid. A company can fail because of a shortage of cash, even while profitable.
- to generate project rate of returns. The time of _________s into and out of projects are used as inputs to financial models such as internal rate of return, and net present value.
- to examine income or growth of a business when it is believed that accrual accounting concepts do not represent economic realities. Alternately, _________ can be used to 'validate' the net income generated by accrual accounting.

_________ as a generic term may be used differently depending on context, and certain _________ definitions may be adapted by analysts and users for their own uses. Common terms include operating _________ and free _________.

_________s can be classified into:

1. Operational _________s: Cash received or expended as a result of the company's core business activities.
2. Investment _________s: Cash received or expended through capital expenditure, investments or acquisitions.
3. Financing _________s: Cash received or expended as a result of financial activities, such as interests and dividends.

All three together - the net _________ - are necessary to reconcile the beginning cash balance to the ending cash balance. Loan draw downs or equity injections, that is just shifting of capital but no expenditure as such, are not considered in the net _________.

a. Real option
b. Corporate finance
c. Shareholder value
d. Cash flow

9. _________ are formal records of a business' financial activities.

_________ provide an overview of a business' financial condition in both short and long term. There are four basic _________:

1. **Balance sheet**: also referred to as statement of financial position or condition, reports on a company's assets, liabilities, and net equity as of a given point in time.
2. **Income statement**: also referred to as Profit and Loss statement (or a 'P'L'), reports on a company's income, expenses, and profits over a period of time.
3. **Statement of retained earnings**: explains the changes in a company's retained earnings over the reporting period.
4. **Statement of cash flows**: reports on a company's cash flow activities, particularly its operating, investing and financing activities.

a. Statement of retained earnings
b. Statement on Auditing Standards No. 70: Service Organizations
c. Notes to the Financial Statements
d. Financial statements

10. In finance, _________ (or gearing) is borrowing money to supplement existing funds for investment in such a way that the potential positive or negative outcome is magnified and/or enhanced. It generally refers to using borrowed funds, or debt, so as to attempt to increase the returns to equity. Deleveraging is the action of reducing borrowings.

a. Financial endowment
b. Pension fund
c. Limited partnership
d. Leverage

11. The term _________ is a term applied to practices that are perfunctory, or seek to satisfy the minimum requirements or to conform to a convention or doctrine. It has different meanings in different fields.

In accounting, _________ earnings are those earnings of companies in addition to actual earnings calculated under the Generally Accepted Accounting Principles (GAAP) in their quarterly and yearly financial reports.

a. Pro forma
b. Long-term liabilities
c. Deferred income
d. Deferred financing costs

12. In accounting, _________ refers to the portion of net income which is retained by the corporation rather than distributed to its owners as dividends. Similarly, if the corporation makes a loss, then that loss is retained and called variously retained losses, accumulated losses or accumulated deficit. _________ and losses are cumulative from year to year with losses offsetting earnings.

a. Generally Accepted Accounting Principles
b. Matching principle
c. Historical cost
d. Retained earnings

13. Accrual, in accounting, describes the accounting method known as _________, whereby revenues and expenses are recognized when they are accrued, i.e. accumulated (earned or incurred), regardless when the actual cash is received or paid out.

E.g. a company delivers a product to a customer who will pay for it 30 days later in the next fiscal year starting a week after the delivery. The company recognizes the proceeds as a revenue in its current income statement still for the fiscal year of the delivery, even though it will get paid in cash during the following accounting period.

a. Accrual basis
b. A Random Walk Down Wall Street
c. ABN Amro
d. AAB

14. In finance, a _________ is the party in a loan agreement which receives money or other instrument from a lender and promises to repay the lender in a specified time.

a. Cash credit
b. Debt management plan
c. Line of credit
d. Borrower

15. _________ are the earnings returned on the initial investment amount.

In the US, the Financial Accounting Standards Board (FASB) requires companies' income statements to report _________ for each of the major categories of the income statement: continuing operations, discontinued operations, extraordinary items, and net income.

The _________ formula does not include preferred dividends for categories outside of continued operations and net income.

a. Earnings per share
b. Average accounting return
c. Inventory turnover
d. Assets turnover

16. Net income is informally called the _________ because it is typically found on the last line of a company's income statement. A related term is top line, meaning revenue, which forms the first line of the account statement.

An equation for net income in merchandising:

Net income or net loss =Revenue - Cost of goods sold - Sales discounts - Sales returns and allowances - Expenses - Minority interest - Preferred stock dividends

a. Net income
b. Retained earnings
c. Bottom line
d. Matching principle

17. _________, refers to consumption opportunity gained by an entity within a specified time frame, which is generally expressed in monetary terms. However, for households and individuals, '_________ is the sum of all the wages, salaries, profits, interests payments, rents and other forms of earnings received... in a given period of time.' For firms, _________ generally refers to net-profit: what remains of revenue after expenses have been subtracted.
a. Income
b. OIBDA
c. Annual report
d. Accrual

18. An _________ is a financial statement for companies that indicates how Revenue is transformed into net income The purpose of the _________ is to show managers and investors whether the company made or lost money during the period being reported.

The important thing to remember about an _________ is that it represents a period of time.

a. ABN Amro
b. AAB
c. Income statement
d. A Random Walk Down Wall Street

19. In business and finance, a _________ (also referred to as equity _________) of stock means a _________ of ownership in a corporation (company.) In the plural, stocks is often used as a synonym for _________s especially in the United States, but it is less commonly used that way outside of North America.

In the United Kingdom, South Africa, and Australia, stock can also refer to completely different financial instruments such as government bonds or, less commonly, to all kinds of marketable securities.

a. Share
b. Procter ' Gamble
c. Bucket shop
d. Margin

20. _________ is typically a higher ranking stock than voting shares, and its terms are negotiated between the corporation and the investor.

_________ usually carry no voting rights, but may carry superior priority over common stock in the payment of dividends and upon liquidation. _________ may carry a dividend that is paid out prior to any dividends to common stock holders.

a. Follow-on offering
b. Trade-off theory
c. Second lien loan
d. Preferred stock

21. _________ is a form of corporation equity ownership represented in the securities. It is dangerous in comparison to preferred shares and some other investment options, in that in the event of bankruptcy, _________ investors receive their funds after preferred stockholders, bondholders, creditors, etc. On the other hand, common shares on average perform better than preferred shares or bonds over time.

a. Stock split
b. Stock market bubble
c. Stop-limit order
d. Common stock

22. In business, _________ is the total assets minus total outside liabilities of an individual or a company. For a company, this is called shareholders' equity and may be referred to as book value. _________ is stated as at a particular point in time.

a. Moneylender
b. Restructuring
c. Certified International Investment Analyst
d. Net worth

23. The _________ is one of the basic financial statements as per Generally Accepted Accounting Principles, and it explains the changes in a company's retained earnings over the reporting period. It breaks down changes affecting the account, such as profits or losses from operations, dividends paid, and any other items charged or credited to retained earnings. A retained earnings statement is required by Generally Accepted Accounting Principles (GAAP) whenever comparative balance sheets and income statements are presented.
a. Financial statements
b. Notes to the Financial Statements
c. Statement on Auditing Standards No. 70: Service Organizations
d. Statement of retained earnings

24. _________ is the difference between price and the costs of bringing to market whatever it is that is accounted as an enterprise (whether by harvest, extraction, manufacture, or purchase) in terms of the component costs of delivered goods and/or services and any operating or other expenses.

A key difficulty in measuring profit is in defining costs. Pure economic monetary profits can be zero or negative even in competitive equilibrium when accounted monetized costs exceed monetized price.

a. Economic profit
b. Accounting profit
c. AAB
d. A Random Walk Down Wall Street

25. In financial accounting, a _________ or statement of cash flows is a financial statement that shows a company's flow of cash. The money coming into the business is called cash inflow, and money going out from the business is called cash outflow. The statement shows how changes in balance sheet and income accounts affect cash and cash equivalents, and breaks the analysis down to operating, investing, and financing activities.
a. 529 plan
b. Cash flow statement
c. 7-Eleven
d. 4-4-5 Calendar

26. _________ is a measure of the ability of a debtor to pay their debts as and when they fall due. It is usually expressed as a ratio or a percentage of current liabilities.

For a corporation with a published balance sheet there are various ratios used to calculate a measure of liquidity.

a. Invested capital
b. Operating leverage
c. Operating profit margin
d. Accounting liquidity

27. In business and accounting, _________s are everything of value that is owned by a person or company. The balance sheet of a firm records the monetary value of the _________s owned by the firm. The two major _________ classes are tangible _________s and intangible _________s.

a. Accounts payable
b. EBITDA
c. Asset
d. Income

28. The _________ is a financial ratio that measures whether or not a firm has enough resources to pay its debts over the next 12 months. It compares a firm's current assets to its current liabilities. It is expressed as follows:

$$\text{Current ratio} = \frac{\text{Current Assets}}{\text{Current Liabilities}}$$

For example, if WXY Company's current assets are $50,000,000 and its current liabilities are $40,000,000, then its _________ would be $50,000,000 divided by $40,000,000, which equals 1.25.

a. Current ratio
b. Debt service coverage ratio
c. Sustainable growth rate
d. PEG ratio

29. In finance, the Acid-test or _________ or liquid ratio measures the ability of a company to use its near cash or quick assets to immediately extinguish or retire its current liabilities. Quick assets include those current assets that presumably can be quickly converted to cash at close to their book values.

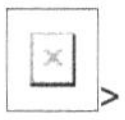

Generally, the acid test ratio should be 1:1 or better, however this varies widely by industry.

a. P/E ratio
b. Net assets
c. Financial ratio
d. Quick ratio

30. The term _________ is often used to refer to the investment management of collective investments, (not necessarily) whilst the more generic fund management may refer to all forms of institutional investment as well as investment management for private investors. Investment managers who specialize in advisory or discretionary management on behalf of (normally wealthy) private investors may often refer to their services as wealth management or portfolio management often within the context of so-called 'private banking'.

The provision of 'investment management services' includes elements of financial analysis, asset selection, stock selection, plan implementation and ongoing monitoring of investments.

a. A Random Walk Down Wall Street
b. ABN Amro
c. AAB
d. Asset management

31. _________ is a list for goods and materials held available in stock by a business. It is also used for a list of the contents of a household and for a list for testamentary purposes of the possessions of someone who has died. In accounting _________ is considered an asset.

a. Inventory
b. AAB
c. ABN Amro
d. A Random Walk Down Wall Street

32. The _________ is an equation that equals the cost of goods sold divided by the average inventory. Average inventory equals beginning inventory plus ending inventory divided by 2.

The formula for _________:

$$\text{Inventory Turnover} = \frac{\text{Cost of Goods Sold}}{\text{Average Inventory}}$$

The formula for average inventory:

$$\text{Average Inventory} = \frac{\text{Beginning inventory+Ending inventory}}{2}$$

A low turnover rate may point to overstocking, obsolescence, or deficiencies in the product line or marketing effort.

a. Earnings yield
b. Information ratio
c. Operating leverage
d. Inventory turnover

33. _________ is one of the Accounting Liquidity ratios, a financial ratio. This ratio measures the number of times, on average, the inventory is sold during the period. Its purpose is to measure the liquidity of the inventory.
a. Inventory turnover ratio
b. ABN Amro
c. A Random Walk Down Wall Street
d. AAB

34. _________ is a business term and may be used as a broad measure of asset efficiency and is calculated by dividing sales revenue by the total assets.

It's also used in the Du Pont Identity:

$$\frac{Net\ Earnings}{Shareholders\ Eq.} = \frac{Net\ Earnings}{Sales(Income)} * \frac{Sales(Income)}{TotalAssets} * \frac{Total\ Assets}{Shareholders\ Eq.}$$

In which,

$$Net\ Margin = \frac{Net\ Earnings}{Sales(Income)}$$
$$Total\ Asset\ Turnover = \frac{Sales(Income)}{TotalAssets}$$
$$Financial\ Leverage = \frac{Average\ Total\ Assets}{Average\ Total\ Equity}$$

The net margin is a summary indicator of an income statement, Asset turnover is an indicator of the left side of the balance sheet (total assets' side) and Leverage is an indicator of the right side of the Balance Sheet (liabilities and shareholders' equity' side.)

The Du Pont Identity helps many companies or individuals, visualize and comprehend the analysis of a financial statement or annual report of a company, in return on assets and return on investments.

a. Invested capital
b. Operating profit margin
c. Earnings yield
d. Assets turnover

35. In accountancy, _________ is a company's average collection period. A low number of days indicates that the company collects its outstanding receivables quickly. Typically, _________ is calculated monthly. The _________ figure is an index of the relationship between outstanding receivables and sales achieved over a given period. The _________ analysis provides general information about the number of days on average that customers take to pay invoices.

a. Round-tripping
b. Residual value
c. Net pay
d. Days sales outstanding

36. _________ plant, and equipment, is a term used in accountancy for assets and property which cannot easily be converted into cash. This can be compared with current assets such as cash or bank accounts, which are described as liquid assets. In most cases, only tangible assets are referred to as fixed.

a. Petty cash
b. Fixed asset
c. Remittance advice
d. Percentage of Completion

37. _________ is that which is owed; usually referencing assets owed, but the term can cover other obligations. In the case of assets, _________ is a means of using future purchasing power in the present before a summation has been earned. Some companies and corporations use _________ as a part of their overall corporate finance strategy.

a. Cross-collateralization
b. Partial Payment
c. Credit cycle
d. Debt

38. In finance, _________ is the process of estimating the potential market value of a financial asset or liability. they can be done on assets (for example, investments in marketable securities such as stocks, options, business enterprises, or intangible assets such as patents and trademarks) or on liabilities (e.g., Bonds issued by a company.) _________s are required in many contexts including investment analysis, capital budgeting, merger and acquisition transactions, financial reporting, taxable events to determine the proper tax liability, and in litigation.

a. Share
b. Valuation
c. Margin
d. Procter ' Gamble

39. _________ is a financial ratio that indicates the percentage of a company's assets are provided via debt. It is the ratio of total debt (the sum of current liabilities and long-term liabilities) and total assets (the sum of current assets, fixed assets, and other assets such as 'goodwill'.)

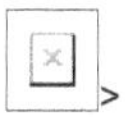

>

or alternatively:

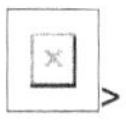

>

For example, a company with $2 million in total assets and $500,000 in total liabilities would have a _________ of 25%

Like all financial ratios, a company's _________ should be compared with their industry average or other competing firms.

a. Cash concentration
b. Cash management
c. Capitalization rate
d. Debt ratio

40. In business and finance accounting, _________ is equal to the gross profit minus overheads minus interest payable plus/minus one off items for a given time period (usually: accounting period.)

A common synonym for '_________' when discussing financial statements (which include a balance sheet and an income statement) is the bottom line. This term results from the traditional appearance of an income statement which shows all allocated revenues and expenses over a specified time period with the resulting summation on the bottom line of the report.

a. Gross sales
b. Deferred
c. Salvage value
d. Net profit

41. Profit margin, net margin, _________ or net profit ratio all refer to a measure of profitability. It is calculated by finding the net profit as a percentage of the revenue.

The profit margin is mostly used for internal comparison.

a. Profit maximization
b. Profit margin
c. 4-4-5 Calendar
d. Net profit margin

42. In finance, a _________ is collateral that the holder of a position in securities, options, or futures contracts has to deposit to cover the credit risk of his counterparty (most often his broker.) This risk can arise if the holder has done any of the following:

- borrowed cash from the counterparty to buy securities or options,
- sold securities or options short, or
- entered into a futures contract.

The collateral can be in the form of cash or securities, and it is deposited in a _________ account. On U.S. futures exchanges, '_________' was formally called performance bond.

_________ buying is buying securities with cash borrowed from a broker, using other securities as collateral.

a. Procter ' Gamble
b. Share
c. Credit
d. Margin

43. _________, Net Margin, Net _________ or Net Profit Ratio all refer to a measure of profitability. It is calculated using a formula and written as a percentage or a number.

$$\text{Net profit margin} = \frac{\text{Net profit after taxes}}{\text{Net Sales}}$$

The _________ is mostly used for internal comparison.

a. Profit maximization
b. Net profit margin
c. 4-4-5 Calendar
d. Profit margin

44. _________ is the price at which an asset would trade in a competitive Walrasian auction setting. _________ is often used interchangeably with open _________, fair value or fair _________, although these terms have distinct definitions in different standards, and may differ in some circumstances.

International Valuation Standards defines _________ as 'the estimated amount for which a property should exchange on the date of valuation between a willing buyer and a willing seller in an arm'e;s-length transaction after proper marketing wherein the parties had each acted knowledgeably, prudently, and without compulsion.'

_________ is a concept distinct from market price, which is 'e;the price at which one can transact'e;, while _________ is 'e;the true underlying value'e; according to theoretical standards.

a. T-Model
b. Wrap account
c. Market value
d. Debt restructuring

45. _________ is the process of comparing the cost, time or quality of what one organization does against what another organization does. The result is often a business case for making changes in order to make improvements.

Also referred to as 'best practice _________' or 'process _________', it is a process used in management and particularly strategic management, in which organizations evaluate various aspects of their processes in relation to best practice, usually within their own sector.

a. 7-Eleven
b. 529 plan
c. 4-4-5 Calendar
d. Benchmarking

46. _________ measures the nominal future sum of money that a given sum of money is 'worth' at a specified time in the future assuming a certain interest rate rate of return; it is the present value multiplied by the accumulation function.

The value does not include corrections for inflation or other factors that affect the true value of money in the future. This is used in time value of money calculations.

a. Discounted cash flow
b. Future value
c. Present value of costs
d. Future-oriented

1. In finance, _________ (or gearing) is borrowing money to supplement existing funds for investment in such a way that the potential positive or negative outcome is magnified and/or enhanced. It generally refers to using borrowed funds, or debt, so as to attempt to increase the returns to equity. Deleveraging is the action of reducing borrowings.

a. Financial endowment
b. Leverage
c. Pension fund
d. Limited partnership

2. In financial accounting, a _________ or statement of financial position is a summary of a person's or organization's balances. Assets, liabilities and ownership equity are listed as of a specific date, such as the end of its financial year. A _________ is often described as a snapshot of a company's financial condition.

a. Statement of retained earnings
b. Statement on Auditing Standards No. 70: Service Organizations
c. Financial statements
d. Balance sheet

3. _________ are formal records of a business' financial activities.

_________ provide an overview of a business' financial condition in both short and long term. There are four basic _________:

1. **Balance sheet**: also referred to as statement of financial position or condition, reports on a company's assets, liabilities, and net equity as of a given point in time.
2. **Income statement**: also referred to as Profit and Loss statement (or a 'P'L'), reports on a company's income, expenses, and profits over a period of time.
3. **Statement of retained earnings**: explains the changes in a company's retained earnings over the reporting period.
4. **Statement of cash flows**: reports on a company's cash flow activities, particularly its operating, investing and financing activities.

a. Statement of retained earnings
b. Statement on Auditing Standards No. 70: Service Organizations
c. Notes to the Financial Statements
d. Financial statements

4. _________, refers to consumption opportunity gained by an entity within a specified time frame, which is generally expressed in monetary terms. However, for households and individuals, '_________ is the sum of all the wages, salaries, profits, interests payments, rents and other forms of earnings received... in a given period of time.' For firms, _________ generally refers to net-profit: what remains of revenue after expenses have been subtracted.

a. Income
b. OIBDA
c. Annual report
d. Accrual

5. An _________ is a financial statement for companies that indicates how Revenue is transformed into net income The purpose of the _________ is to show managers and investors whether the company made or lost money during the period being reported.

The important thing to remember about an _________ is that it represents a period of time.

a. AAB
b. A Random Walk Down Wall Street
c. ABN Amro
d. Income statement

6. _________ or financing is to provide capital (funds), which means money for a project, a person, a business or any other private or public institutions.

Those funds can be allocated for either short term or long term purposes. The health fund is a new way of _________ private healthcare centers.

a. Funding
b. Proxy fight
c. Product life cycle
d. Synthetic CDO

7. In business and accounting, _________s are everything of value that is owned by a person or company. The balance sheet of a firm records the monetary value of the _________s owned by the firm. The two major _________ classes are tangible _________s and intangible _________s.

a. Accounts payable
b. EBITDA
c. Asset
d. Income

8. _________, in microeconomics, are the cost advantages that a business obtains due to expansion. _________ may be utilized by any size firm expanding its scale of operation.

a. Articles of incorporation
b. Economies of scale
c. Employee Retirement Income Security Act
d. Uniform Commercial Code

9. In economics, business, and accounting, a _________ is the value of money that has been used up to produce something, and hence is not available for use anymore. In business, the _________ may be one of acquisition, in which case the amount of money expended to acquire it is counted as _________. In this case, money is the input that is gone in order to acquire the thing.
a. Sliding scale fees
b. Fixed costs
c. Marginal cost
d. Cost

10. The _________ is a measure of how revenue growth translates into growth in operating income. It is a measure of leverage, and of how risky (volatile) a company's operating income is.

There are various measures of _________, which can be interpreted analogously to financial leverage.

a. Average accounting return
b. Operating leverage
c. Asset turnover
d. Invested capital

11. The institution most often referenced by the word '_________' is a public or publicly traded _________, the shares of which are traded on a public stock exchange (e.g., the New York Stock Exchange or Nasdaq in the United States) where shares of stock of _________s are bought and sold by and to the general public. Most of the largest businesses in the world are publicly traded _________s. However, the majority of _________s are said to be closely held, privately held or close _________s, meaning that no ready market exists for the trading of shares.
a. Depository Trust Company
b. Protect
c. Federal Home Loan Mortgage Corporation
d. Corporation

12. The term _________ is a term applied to practices that are perfunctory, or seek to satisfy the minimum requirements or to conform to a convention or doctrine. It has different meanings in different fields.

In accounting, _________ earnings are those earnings of companies in addition to actual earnings calculated under the Generally Accepted Accounting Principles (GAAP) in their quarterly and yearly financial reports.

a. Pro forma
b. Long-term liabilities
c. Deferred income
d. Deferred financing costs

1. A _________ is a fungible, negotiable instrument representing financial value. They are broadly categorized into debt securities (such as banknotes, bonds and debentures), and equity securities; e.g., common stocks. The company or other entity issuing the _________ is called the issuer.
   a. Security
   b. Securities lending
   c. Book entry
   d. Tracking stock

2. _________ can be regarded as an outcome of mental processes (cognitive process) leading to the selection of a course of action among several alternatives. Every _________ process produces a final choice. The output can be an action or an opinion of choice.
   a. Decision making
   b. 7-Eleven
   c. 4-4-5 Calendar
   d. 529 plan

3. In finance, _________ (or gearing) is borrowing money to supplement existing funds for investment in such a way that the potential positive or negative outcome is magnified and/or enhanced. It generally refers to using borrowed funds, or debt, so as to attempt to increase the returns to equity. Deleveraging is the action of reducing borrowings.
   a. Limited partnership
   b. Financial endowment
   c. Pension fund
   d. Leverage

4. _________ is a fee paid on borrowed assets. It is the price paid for the use of borrowed money , or, money earned by deposited funds . Assets that are sometimes lent with _________ include money, shares, consumer goods through hire purchase, major assets such as aircraft, and even entire factories in finance lease arrangements.
   a. Interest
   b. A Random Walk Down Wall Street
   c. Insolvency
   d. AAB

5. An _________ is the price a borrower pays for the use of money they do not own, and the return a lender receives for deferring the use of funds, by lending it to the borrower. _________s are normally expressed as a percentage rate over the period of one year.

_________s targets are also a vital tool of monetary policy and are used to control variables like investment, inflation, and unemployment.

a. Interest rate
b. ABN Amro
c. A Random Walk Down Wall Street
d. AAB

6. _________ is the concept of adding accumulated interest back to the principal, so that interest is earned on interest from that moment on. The act of declaring interest to be principal is called compounding (i.e., interest is compounded.) A loan, for example, may have its interest compounded every month: in this case, a loan with $100 principal and 1% interest per month would have a balance of $101 at the end of the first month.
a. Penny stock
b. Compound interest
c. 4-4-5 Calendar
d. Risk management

7. _________ measures the nominal future sum of money that a given sum of money is 'worth' at a specified time in the future assuming a certain interest rate rate of return; it is the present value multiplied by the accumulation function.

The value does not include corrections for inflation or other factors that affect the true value of money in the future. This is used in time value of money calculations.

a. Present value of costs
b. Future-oriented
c. Discounted cash flow
d. Future value

8. A '_________' is a 'Charge' that is paid to obtain the right to delay a payment. Essentially, the payer purchases the right to make a given payment in the future instead of in the Present. The '_________', or 'Charge' that must be paid to delay the payment, is simply the difference between what the payment amount would be if it were paid in the present and what the payment amount would be paid if it were paid in the future.
a. Discount
b. Value at risk
c. Risk modeling
d. Risk aversion

9. _________ is the value on a given date of a future payment or series of future payments, discounted to reflect the time value of money and other factors such as investment risk. _________ calculations are widely used in business and economics to provide a means to compare cash flows at different times on a meaningful 'like to like' basis.

The most commonly applied model of the time value of money is compound interest.

a. Net present value
b. Negative gearing
c. Present value of benefits
d. Present value

10. In economics, business, and accounting, a _________ is the value of money that has been used up to produce something, and hence is not available for use anymore. In business, the _________ may be one of acquisition, in which case the amount of money expended to acquire it is counted as _________. In this case, money is the input that is gone in order to acquire the thing.

a. Cost
b. Marginal cost
c. Sliding scale fees
d. Fixed costs

11. An _________ can be defined as a contract which provides an income stream in return for an initial payment.

An immediate _________ is an _________ for which the time between the contract date and the date of the first payment is not longer than the time interval between payments. A common use for an immediate _________ is to provide a pension to a retired person or persons.

a. Amortization
b. Intrinsic value
c. AT'T Inc.
d. Annuity

12. A _________ is an annuity in which the periodic payments begin on a fixed date and continue indefinitely. It is sometimes referred to as a perpetual annuity. Fixed coupon payments on permanently invested (irredeemable) sums of money are prime examples of these. Scholarships paid perpetually from an endowment fit the definition of _________.

a. Stochastic volatility
b. Perpetuity
c. LIBOR market model
d. Current yield

13. _________ is the balance of the amounts of cash being received and paid by a business during a defined period of time, sometimes tied to a specific project. Measurement of _________ can be used

- to evaluate the state or performance of a business or project.
- to determine problems with liquidity. Being profitable does not necessarily mean being liquid. A company can fail because of a shortage of cash, even while profitable.
- to generate project rate of returns. The time of _________s into and out of projects are used as inputs to financial models such as internal rate of return, and net present value.
- to examine income or growth of a business when it is believed that accrual accounting concepts do not represent economic realities. Alternately, _________ can be used to 'validate' the net income generated by accrual accounting.

_________ as a generic term may be used differently depending on context, and certain _________ definitions may be adapted by analysts and users for their own uses. Common terms include operating _________ and free _________.

_________s can be classified into:

1. Operational _________s: Cash received or expended as a result of the company's core business activities.
2. Investment _________s: Cash received or expended through capital expenditure, investments or acquisitions.
3. Financing _________s: Cash received or expended as a result of financial activities, such as interests and dividends.

All three together - the net _________ - are necessary to reconcile the beginning cash balance to the ending cash balance. Loan draw downs or equity injections, that is just shifting of capital but no expenditure as such, are not considered in the net _________.

a. Cash flow
b. Real option
c. Shareholder value
d. Corporate finance

14. The _________, effective annual interest rate, Annual Equivalent Rate (AER) or simply effective rate is the interest rate on a loan or financial product restated from the nominal interest rate as an interest rate with annual compound interest. It is used to compare the annual interest between loans with different compounding terms (daily, monthly, annually, or other.)

The _________ differs in two important respects from the annual percentage rate (APR):

1. the _________ generally does not incorporate one-time charges such as front-end fees;
2. the _________ is (generally) not defined by legal or regulatory authorities (as APR is in many jurisdictions.)

By contrast, the 'effective APR' is used as a legal term, where front-fees and other costs can be included, as defined by local law.

Annual Percentage Yield or effective annual yield is the analogous concept used for savings or investment products, such as a certificate of deposit.

a. AAB
b. A Random Walk Down Wall Street
c. ABN Amro
d. Effective interest rate

15. _________ expresses an annual rate of interest taking into account the effect of compounding, usually for deposit or investment products (such as a certificate of deposit.) It is analogous to the Annual percentage rate (APR), which is used for loans. In some jurisdictions, the use and definition of _________ may be regulated by a government agency, in which case it would generally be capitalized.

a. ABN Amro
b. AAB
c. A Random Walk Down Wall Street
d. Annual percentage yield

16. In finance, the term _________ describes the amount in cash that returns to the owners of a security. Normally it does not include the price variations, at the difference of the total return. _________ applies to various stated rates of return on stocks (common and preferred, and convertible), fixed income instruments (bonds, notes, bills, strips, zero coupon), and some other investment type insurance products (e.g. annuities.)

a. Yield
b. Macaulay duration
c. 4-4-5 Calendar
d. Yield to maturity

17. _________ is the process of decreasing an amount over a period of time. The word comes from Middle English amortisen to kill, alienate in mortmain, from Anglo-French amorteser, alteration of amortir, from Vulgar Latin admortire to kill, from Latin ad- + mort-, mors death. Particular instances of the term include:

- _________ (business), the allocation of a lump sum amount to different time periods, particularly for loans and other forms of finance, including related interest or other finance charges.
  - _________ schedule, a table detailing each periodic payment on a loan (typically a mortgage), as generated by an _________ calculator.
  - Negative _________, an _________ schedule where the loan amount actually increases through not paying the full interest
- Amortized analysis, analyzing the execution cost of algorithms over a sequence of operations.
- _________ of capital expenditures of certain assets under accounting rules, particularly intangible assets, in a manner analogous to depreciation.
- _________ (tax law)

_________ is also used in the context of zoning regulations and describes the time in which a property owner has to relocate when the property's use constitutes a preexisting nonconforming use under zoning regulations.

- Depreciation

.

a. AT'T Inc.
b. Option
c. Intrinsic value
d. Amortization

18. An _________ is a table detailing each periodic payment on a amortizing loan (typically a mortgage), as generated by an amortization calculator.

While a portion of every payment is applied towards both the interest and the principal balance of the loan, the exact amount applied to principal each time varies (with the remainder going to interest.) An _________ reveals the specific monetary amount put towards interest, as well as the specific put towards the Principal balance, with each payment.

a. Adjusting entries
b. Annual report
c. Adjusted basis
d. Amortization schedule

19. The terms _________ , nominal _________, and effective _________ describe the interest rate for a whole year (annualized), rather than just a monthly fee/rate, as applied on a loan, mortgage, credit card, etc. Those terms have formal, legal definitions in some countries or legal jurisdictions, but in general:

- The nominal _________ is the simple-interest rate (for a year.)
- The effective _________ is the fee+compound interest rate (calculated across a year.)

The nominal _________ is calculated as: the rate, for a payment period, multiplied by the number of payment periods in a year. However, the exact legal definition of 'effective _________' can vary greatly in each jurisdiction, depending on the type of fees included, such as participation fees, loan origination fees, monthly service charges, or late fees. The effective _________ has been called the 'mathematically-true' interest rate for each year. The computation for the effective _________, as the fee+compound interest rate, can also vary depending on whether the up-front fees, such as origination or participation fees, are added to the entire amount, or treated as a short-term loan due in the first payment.

a. A Random Walk Down Wall Street
b. ABN Amro
c. Annual percentage rate
d. AAB

20. In finance, the value of an option consists of two components, its intrinsic value and its _________. Time value is simply the difference between option value and intrinsic value. _________ is also known as theta, extrinsic value, or instrumental value.
a. Conservatism
b. Debt buyer
c. Time value
d. Global Squeeze

21. Simply put, _________ is the value of money figuring in a given amount of interest for a given amount of time. For example 100 dollars of todays money held for a year at 5 percent interest is worth 105 dollars, therefore 100 dollars paid now or 105 dollars paid exactly one year from now is the same amount of payment of money with that given intersest at that given amount of time. This notion dates at least to Martín de Azpilcueta of the School of Salamanca.

All of the standard calculations for _________ derive from the most basic algebraic expression for the present value of a future sum, 'discounted' to the present by an amount equal to the _________. For example, a sum of FV to be received in one year is discounted (at the rate of interest r) to give a sum of PV at present: PV = FV -- rÂ·PV = FV/(1+r).

a. Time value of money
b. Coefficient of variation
c. Zero-coupon bond
d. Current account

22. _________ is the provision of resources (such as granting a loan) by one party to another party where that second party does not reimburse the first party immediately, thereby generating a debt, and instead arranges either to repay or return those resources (or material(s) of equal value) at a later date. The first party is called a creditor, also known as a lender, while the second party is called a debtor, also known as a borrower.

Movements of financial capital are normally dependent on either _________ or equity transfers.

a. Clearing house
b. Comparable
c. Warrant
d. Credit

23. In economics, the concept of the _________ refers to the decision-making time frame of a firm in which at least one factor of production is fixed. Costs which are fixed in the _________ have no impact on a firms decisions. For example a firm can raise output by increasing the amount of labour through overtime.

a. 4-4-5 Calendar
b. Long-run
c. 529 plan
d. Short-run

1. _________ mature in one year or less. Like zero-coupon bonds, they do not pay interest prior to maturity; instead they are sold at a discount of the par value to create a positive yield to maturity. Many regard _________ as the least risky investment available to U.S. investors.

a. Treasury securities
b. 4-4-5 Calendar
c. Treasury bills
d. Treasury Inflation Protected Securities

2. In finance, a _________ is a debt security, in which the authorized issuer owes the holders a debt and, depending on the terms of the _________, is obliged to pay interest (the coupon) and/or to repay the principal at a later date, termed maturity.

Thus a _________ is a loan: the issuer is the borrower, the _________ holder is the lender, and the coupon is the interest. _________s provide the borrower with external funds to finance long-term investments, or, in the case of government _________s, to finance current expenditure.

a. Convertible bond
b. Catastrophe bonds
c. Puttable bond
d. Bond

3. _________ is a fee paid on borrowed assets. It is the price paid for the use of borrowed money , or, money earned by deposited funds . Assets that are sometimes lent with _________ include money, shares, consumer goods through hire purchase, major assets such as aircraft, and even entire factories in finance lease arrangements.

a. A Random Walk Down Wall Street
b. AAB
c. Insolvency
d. Interest

4. An _________ is the price a borrower pays for the use of money they do not own, and the return a lender receives for deferring the use of funds, by lending it to the borrower. _________s are normally expressed as a percentage rate over the period of one year.

_________s targets are also a vital tool of monetary policy and are used to control variables like investment, inflation, and unemployment.

a. A Random Walk Down Wall Street
b. AAB
c. Interest rate
d. ABN Amro

5. In finance, _________ is the process of estimating the potential market value of a financial asset or liability. they can be done on assets (for example, investments in marketable securities such as stocks, options, business enterprises, or intangible assets such as patents and trademarks) or on liabilities (e.g., Bonds issued by a company.) _________s are required in many contexts including investment analysis, capital budgeting, merger and acquisition transactions, financial reporting, taxable events to determine the proper tax liability, and in litigation.
a. Share
b. Procter ' Gamble
c. Margin
d. Valuation

6. In finance, the _________ of a financial asset measures the sensitivity of the asset's price to interest rate movements, expressed as a number of years. The reason for expressing this sensitivity in years is that the time that will elapse until a cash flow is received allows more interest to accumulate. Therefore the price of an asset with long term cashflows has more interest rate sensitivity than an asset with cashflows in the near future.
a. Yield to maturity
b. Duration
c. Macaulay duration
d. 4-4-5 Calendar

7. _________ is an economic concept with commonplace familiarity. It is the price that a good or service is offered at, or will fetch, in the marketplace. It is of interest mainly in the study of microeconomics.
a. Central Securities Depository
b. Market price
c. Convertible arbitrage
d. Delta hedging

8. In economics, business, and accounting, a _________ is the value of money that has been used up to produce something, and hence is not available for use anymore. In business, the _________ may be one of acquisition, in which case the amount of money expended to acquire it is counted as _________. In this case, money is the input that is gone in order to acquire the thing.

a. Marginal cost
b. Sliding scale fees
c. Fixed costs
d. Cost

9. In business and accounting, _________s are everything of value that is owned by a person or company. The balance sheet of a firm records the monetary value of the _________s owned by the firm. The two major _________ classes are tangible _________s and intangible _________s.
a. Accounts payable
b. Asset
c. EBITDA
d. Income

10. In finance, the term _________ describes the amount in cash that returns to the owners of a security. Normally it does not include the price variations, at the difference of the total return. _________ applies to various stated rates of return on stocks (common and preferred, and convertible), fixed income instruments (bonds, notes, bills, strips, zero coupon), and some other investment type insurance products (e.g. annuities.)
a. Yield
b. Macaulay duration
c. 4-4-5 Calendar
d. Yield to maturity

11. A '_________' is a 'Charge' that is paid to obtain the right to delay a payment. Essentially, the payer purchases the right to make a given payment in the future instead of in the Present. The '_________', or 'Charge' that must be paid to delay the payment, is simply the difference between what the payment amount would be if it were paid in the present and what the payment amount would be paid if it were paid in the future.
a. Risk modeling
b. Value at risk
c. Discount
d. Risk aversion

12. A _________ is a bond bought at a price lower than its face value, with the face value repaid at the time of maturity. It does not make periodic interest payments, or so-called 'coupons,' hence the term zero-coupon bond. Investors earn return from the compounded interest all paid at maturity plus the difference between the discounted price of the bond and its par value.

a. Callable bond
b. Bowie bonds
c. Zero coupon bond
d. Municipal bond

13. A _________ is a generic term for any bond selling for more than 100% of par value, i.e., at a price greater than 100.00, which typically occurs for high coupon bonds in a falling interest rate climate.
a. Premium bond
b. Revenue bonds
c. Nominal yield
d. Municipal bond

14. _________ is a life of security. It may also refer to the final payment date of a loan or other financial instrument, at which point all remaining interest and principal is due to be paid.

1, 3, 6 months _________ band can be calculated by using 30-day per month periods.

a. False billing
b. Primary market
c. Replacement cost
d. Maturity

15. In finance, _________, also known as return on investment is the ratio of money gained or lost on an investment relative to the amount of money invested. The amount of money gained or lost may be referred to as interest, profit/loss, gain/loss, or net income/loss. The money invested may be referred to as the asset, capital, principal, or the cost basis of the investment.
a. Composiition of Creditors
b. Rate of return
c. Stock or scrip dividends
d. Doctrine of the Proper Law

16. The _________ or redemption yield is the yield promised to the bondholder on the assumption that the bond or other fixed-interest security such as gilts will be held to maturity, that all coupon and principal payments will be made and coupon payments are reinvested at the bond's promised yield at the same rate as invested. It is a measure of the return of the bond. This technique in theory allows investors to calculate the fair value of different financial instruments.

a. Yield
b. 4-4-5 Calendar
c. Macaulay duration
d. Yield to maturity

17. _________ is the concept of adding accumulated interest back to the principal, so that interest is earned on interest from that moment on. The act of declaring interest to be principal is called compounding (i.e., interest is compounded.) A loan, for example, may have its interest compounded every month: in this case, a loan with $100 principal and 1% interest per month would have a balance of $101 at the end of the first month.
a. 4-4-5 Calendar
b. Penny stock
c. Risk management
d. Compound interest

18. _________ is the risk (variability in value) borne by an interest-bearing asset, such as a loan or a bond, due to variability of interest rates. In general, as rates rise, the price of a fixed rate bond will fall, and vice versa. _________ is commonly measured by the bond's duration.
a. Official bank rate
b. International Fisher effect
c. A Random Walk Down Wall Street
d. Interest rate risk

19. In business and finance, a _________ (also referred to as equity _________) of stock means a _________ of ownership in a corporation (company.) In the plural, stocks is often used as a synonym for _________s especially in the United States, but it is less commonly used that way outside of North America.

In the United Kingdom, South Africa, and Australia, stock can also refer to completely different financial instruments such as government bonds or, less commonly, to all kinds of marketable securities.

a. Bucket shop
b. Procter ' Gamble
c. Margin
d. Share

20. A _________ is a private or public market for the trading of company stock and derivatives of company stock at an agreed price; these are securities listed on a stock exchange as well as those only traded privately.

The size of the world _________ is estimated at about $36.6 trillion US at the beginning of October 2008 . The world derivatives market has been estimated at about $480 trillion face or nominal value, 12 times the size of the entire world economy.

a. Adolph Coors
b. Anton Gelonkin
c. Andrew Tobias
d. Stock market

21. A _________ is a profit that results from investments into a capital asset, such as stocks, bonds or real estate, which exceeds the purchase price. It is the difference between a higher selling price and a lower purchase price, resulting in a financial gain for the seller. Conversely, a capital loss arises if the proceeds from the sale of a capital asset are less than the purchase price.

a. Capital gain
b. Tax brackets
c. Payroll tax
d. Capital gains tax

22. In finance, _________ refers to the value of a security which is intrinsic to or contained in the security itself. It is also frequently called fundamental value. It is ordinarily calculated by summing the future income generated by the asset, and discounting it to the present value.

a. Alpha
b. Amortization
c. Intrinsic value
d. Accretion

23. _________, in bookkeeping, refers to assets, liabilities, income, and expenses recorded on individual pages of the so called book of final entry or ledger. Changes in _________ value are made by chronologically posting debit (DR) and credit (CR) entries to its page. Examples of _________s are cash, _________s receivable, mortgages, loans, land and buildings, common stock, sales, services provided, wages, and payroll overhead.

a. Account
b. Alpha
c. Accretion
d. Option

24. The coupon or _________ of a bond is the amount of interest paid per year expressed as a percentage of the face value of the bond.

For example if you hold $10,000 nominal of a bond described as a 4.5% loan stock, you will receive $450 in interest each year (probably in two installments of $225 each.)

Not all bonds have coupons.

a. Puttable bond
b. Zero-coupon bond
c. Revenue bonds
d. Coupon rate

25. In finance, _________ are stocks that appreciate in value and yield a high return on equity (ROE.) Analysts compute ROE by taking the company's net income and dividing it by the company's equity. To be classified as a growth stock, analysts expect to see at least 15 percent return on equity.

a. 4-4-5 Calendar
b. Stock valuation
c. Growth stocks
d. Security Analysis

26. _________ is a theory that all economic activities and policies should be oriented towards achieving a state of equilibrium, a steady state.

The theory asserts that the continuous growth model is inherently unstable resulting in a 'boom/bust' cycle, and that continuous growth in the context of finite resources is unlikely to support current levels of prosperity indefinitely.

Proponents of this theory also explicitly challenge the popular equation of economic growth with progress - an equation they have labelled Growth Fetish - and posit that sustainability has inherent value.

a. 4-4-5 Calendar
b. 529 plan
c. 7-Eleven
d. Zero growth

27. A _________ is the price of a single share of a no. of saleable stocks of the company. Once the stock is purchased, the owner becomes a shareholder of the company that issued the share.

a. Trading curb
b. Stock split
c. Share price
d. Whisper numbers

1. A _________ is a private or public market for the trading of company stock and derivatives of company stock at an agreed price; these are securities listed on a stock exchange as well as those only traded privately.

The size of the world _________ is estimated at about $36.6 trillion US at the beginning of October 2008 . The world derivatives market has been estimated at about $480 trillion face or nominal value, 12 times the size of the entire world economy.

a. Adolph Coors
b. Stock market
c. Anton Gelonkin
d. Andrew Tobias

2. In probability theory and statistics, a _________ identifies either the probability of each value of an unidentified random variable (when the variable is discrete), or the probability of the value falling within a particular interval (when the variable is continuous.) The _________ describes the range of possible values that a random variable can attain and the probability that the value of the random variable is within any (measurable) subset of that range. The Normal distribution, often called the 'bell curve'

When the random variable takes values in the set of real numbers, the _________ is completely described by the cumulative distribution function, whose value at each real x is the probability that the random variable is smaller than or equal to x.

a. P-value
b. Standard deviation
c. Probability distribution
d. Correlation

3. In finance, _________, also known as return on investment is the ratio of money gained or lost on an investment relative to the amount of money invested. The amount of money gained or lost may be referred to as interest, profit/loss, gain/loss, or net income/loss. The money invested may be referred to as the asset, capital, principal, or the cost basis of the investment.
a. Doctrine of the Proper Law
b. Stock or scrip dividends
c. Composiition of Creditors
d. Rate of return

4. In probability and statistics, the _________ of a collection of numbers is a measure of the dispersion of the numbers from their expected (mean) value. It can apply to a probability distribution, a random variable, a population or a data set. The _________ is usually denoted with the letter σ (lowercase sigma.)

a. Kurtosis
b. Sample size
c. Mean
d. Standard deviation

5. _________ is the concept of adding accumulated interest back to the principal, so that interest is earned on interest from that moment on. The act of declaring interest to be principal is called compounding (i.e., interest is compounded.) A loan, for example, may have its interest compounded every month: in this case, a loan with $100 principal and 1% interest per month would have a balance of $101 at the end of the first month.

a. 4-4-5 Calendar
b. Compound interest
c. Penny stock
d. Risk management

6. In probability theory and statistics, the _________ of a random variable, probability distribution averaging the squared distance of its possible values from the expected value (mean.) Whereas the mean is a way to describe the location of a distribution, the _________ is a way to capture its scale or degree of being spread out. The unit of _________ is the square of the unit of the original variable.

a. Semivariance
b. Harmonic mean
c. Monte Carlo methods
d. Variance

7. In probability theory and statistics, the _________ is a normalized measure of dispersion of a probability distribution. It is defined as the ratio of the standard deviation 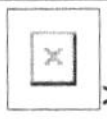> to the mean >:

>

This is only defined for non-zero mean, and is most useful for variables that are always positive. It is also known as unitized risk.

a. Harmonic mean
b. Sample size
c. Random variables
d. Coefficient of variation

8. _________ is a concept in economics, finance, and psychology related to the behaviour of consumers and investors under uncertainty. _________ is the reluctance of a person to accept a bargain with an uncertain payoff rather than another bargain with a more certain, but possibly lower, expected payoff.

The inverse of a person's _________ is sometimes called their risk tolerance

a. Risk premium
b. Risk adjusted return on capital
c. Discount factor
d. Risk aversion

9.

In finance, the _________ can be the expected rate of return above the risk-free interest rate. When measuring risk, a common sense approach is to compare the risk-free return on T-bills and the very risky return on other investments. The difference between these two returns can be interpreted as a measure of the excess return on the average risky asset. This excess return is known as the _________.

a. Risk adjusted return on capital
b. Risk aversion
c. Risk modeling
d. Risk premium

10. The _________ is the weighted-average most likely outcome in gambling, probability theory, economics or finance.

In gambling and probability theory, there is usually a discrete set of possible outcomes. In this case, _________ is a measure of the relative balance of win or loss weighted by their chances of occurring.

a. AAB
b. ABN Amro
c. A Random Walk Down Wall Street
d. Expected return

11. In probability theory and statistics, _________ indicates the strength and direction of a linear relationship between two random variables. That is in contrast with the usage of the term in colloquial speech, which denotes any relationship, not necessarily linear. In general statistical usage, _________ or co-relation refers to the departure of two random variables from independence.

a. Probability distribution
b. Correlation
c. Geometric mean
d. Variance

12. _________ is a list for goods and materials held available in stock by a business. It is also used for a list of the contents of a household and for a list for testamentary purposes of the possessions of someone who has died. In accounting _________ is considered an asset.
a. A Random Walk Down Wall Street
b. AAB
c. ABN Amro
d. Inventory

13. _________ is the risk that the value of an investment will decrease due to moves in market factors. The five standard _________ factors are:

- Equity risk, the risk that stock prices will change.
- Interest rate risk, the risk that interest rates will change.
- Currency risk, the risk that foreign exchange rates will change.
- Commodity risk, the risk that commodity prices (e.g. grains, metals) will change.

As with other forms of risk, _________ may be measured in a number of ways. Traditionally, this is done using a Value at Risk methodology. Value at risk is well established as a risk management technique, but it contains a number of limiting assumptions that constrain its accuracy.

a. Currency risk
b. Transaction risk
c. Market risk
d. Tracking error

14. In business and accounting, _________s are everything of value that is owned by a person or company. The balance sheet of a firm records the monetary value of the _________s owned by the firm. The two major _________ classes are tangible _________s and intangible _________s.
a. Accounts payable
b. EBITDA
c. Income
d. Asset

15. In finance, _________ is the process of estimating the potential market value of a financial asset or liability. they can be done on assets (for example, investments in marketable securities such as stocks, options, business enterprises, or intangible assets such as patents and trademarks) or on liabilities (e.g., Bonds issued by a company.) _________s are required in many contexts including investment analysis, capital budgeting, merger and acquisition transactions, financial reporting, taxable events to determine the proper tax liability, and in litigation.

a. Procter ' Gamble
b. Share
c. Margin
d. Valuation

16. _________ is a fee paid on borrowed assets. It is the price paid for the use of borrowed money , or, money earned by deposited funds . Assets that are sometimes lent with _________ include money, shares, consumer goods through hire purchase, major assets such as aircraft, and even entire factories in finance lease arrangements.

a. AAB
b. Interest
c. Insolvency
d. A Random Walk Down Wall Street

17. An _________ is the price a borrower pays for the use of money they do not own, and the return a lender receives for deferring the use of funds, by lending it to the borrower. _________s are normally expressed as a percentage rate over the period of one year.

_________s targets are also a vital tool of monetary policy and are used to control variables like investment, inflation, and unemployment.

a. A Random Walk Down Wall Street
b. AAB
c. Interest rate
d. ABN Amro

18. The _________, in terms of finance and investing, describes how the expected return of a stock or portfolio is correlated to the return of the financial market as a whole.

An asset with a beta of 0 means that its price is not at all correlated with the market; that asset is independent. A positive beta means that the asset generally follows the market.

a. Current yield
b. Perpetuity
c. LIBOR market model
d. Beta coefficient

19. In economics, _________ is a rise in the general level of prices of goods and services in an economy over a period of time. The term '_________' once referred to increases in the money supply (monetary _________); however, economic debates about the relationship between money supply and price levels have led to its primary use today in describing price _________. _________ can also be described as a decline in the real value of money--a loss of purchasing power in the medium of exchange which is also the monetary unit of account.
a. AAB
b. ABN Amro
c. A Random Walk Down Wall Street
d. Inflation

20. A _________ is the price of a single share of a no. of saleable stocks of the company. Once the stock is purchased, the owner becomes a shareholder of the company that issued the share.
a. Whisper numbers
b. Share price
c. Stock split
d. Trading curb

21. A _________ is a fungible, negotiable instrument representing financial value. They are broadly categorized into debt securities (such as banknotes, bonds and debentures), and equity securities; e.g., common stocks. The company or other entity issuing the _________ is called the issuer.
a. Securities lending
b. Book entry
c. Tracking stock
d. Security

22. In statistics, regression analysis is a collective name for techniques for the modeling and analysis of numerical data consisting of values of a dependent variable and of one or more independent variables The dependent variable in the _________ is modeled as a function of the independent variables, corresponding parameters, and an error term. The error term is treated as a random variable.

a. Regression equation
b. 529 plan
c. 4-4-5 Calendar
d. 7-Eleven

1. In finance, a _________ is a debt security, in which the authorized issuer owes the holders a debt and, depending on the terms of the _________, is obliged to pay interest (the coupon) and/or to repay the principal at a later date, termed maturity.

Thus a _________ is a loan: the issuer is the borrower, the _________ holder is the lender, and the coupon is the interest. _________s provide the borrower with external funds to finance long-term investments, or, in the case of government _________s, to finance current expenditure.

a. Catastrophe bonds
b. Bond
c. Puttable bond
d. Convertible bond

2. _________ is the process of determining the fair price of a bond. As with any security or capital investment, the fair value of a bond is the present value of the stream of cash flows it is expected to generate. Hence, the price or value of a bond is determined by discounting the bond's expected cash flows to the present using the appropriate discount rate.
a. Catastrophe bonds
b. Bond valuation
c. Collateralized debt obligations
d. Bond fund

3. The institution most often referenced by the word '_________' is a public or publicly traded _________, the shares of which are traded on a public stock exchange (e.g., the New York Stock Exchange or Nasdaq in the United States) where shares of stock of _________s are bought and sold by and to the general public. Most of the largest businesses in the world are publicly traded _________s. However, the majority of _________s are said to be closely held, privately held or close _________s, meaning that no ready market exists for the trading of shares.
a. Federal Home Loan Mortgage Corporation
b. Depository Trust Company
c. Corporation
d. Protect

4. _________ is a fee paid on borrowed assets. It is the price paid for the use of borrowed money , or, money earned by deposited funds . Assets that are sometimes lent with _________ include money, shares, consumer goods through hire purchase, major assets such as aircraft, and even entire factories in finance lease arrangements.
a. AAB
b. Interest
c. Insolvency
d. A Random Walk Down Wall Street

5. _________ is that which is owed; usually referencing assets owed, but the term can cover other obligations. In the case of assets, _________ is a means of using future purchasing power in the present before a summation has been earned. Some companies and corporations use _________ as a part of their overall corporate finance strategy.

a. Credit cycle
b. Partial Payment
c. Cross-collateralization
d. Debt

6. In finance, _________ is the process of estimating the potential market value of a financial asset or liability. they can be done on assets (for example, investments in marketable securities such as stocks, options, business enterprises, or intangible assets such as patents and trademarks) or on liabilities (e.g., Bonds issued by a company.) _________s are required in many contexts including investment analysis, capital budgeting, merger and acquisition transactions, financial reporting, taxable events to determine the proper tax liability, and in litigation.

a. Procter ' Gamble
b. Share
c. Margin
d. Valuation

7. In finance, the term _________ describes the amount in cash that returns to the owners of a security. Normally it does not include the price variations, at the difference of the total return. _________ applies to various stated rates of return on stocks (common and preferred, and convertible), fixed income instruments (bonds, notes, bills, strips, zero coupon), and some other investment type insurance products (e.g. annuities.)

a. Macaulay duration
b. Yield to maturity
c. Yield
d. 4-4-5 Calendar

8. In finance, _________, also known as return on investment is the ratio of money gained or lost on an investment relative to the amount of money invested. The amount of money gained or lost may be referred to as interest, profit/loss, gain/loss, or net income/loss. The money invested may be referred to as the asset, capital, principal, or the cost basis of the investment.

a. Rate of return
b. Composiition of Creditors
c. Stock or scrip dividends
d. Doctrine of the Proper Law

9. In financial accounting, a _________ or statement of financial position is a summary of a person's or organization's balances. Assets, liabilities and ownership equity are listed as of a specific date, such as the end of its financial year. A _________ is often described as a snapshot of a company's financial condition.

a. Financial statements
b. Statement on Auditing Standards No. 70: Service Organizations
c. Statement of retained earnings
d. Balance sheet

10. In business and accounting, _________s are everything of value that is owned by a person or company. The balance sheet of a firm records the monetary value of the _________s owned by the firm. The two major _________ classes are tangible _________s and intangible _________s.
a. Income
b. EBITDA
c. Accounts payable
d. Asset

11. In economics, business, and accounting, a _________ is the value of money that has been used up to produce something, and hence is not available for use anymore. In business, the _________ may be one of acquisition, in which case the amount of money expended to acquire it is counted as _________. In this case, money is the input that is gone in order to acquire the thing.
a. Sliding scale fees
b. Fixed costs
c. Marginal cost
d. Cost

12. _________ is typically a higher ranking stock than voting shares, and its terms are negotiated between the corporation and the investor.

_________ usually carry no voting rights, but may carry superior priority over common stock in the payment of dividends and upon liquidation. _________ may carry a dividend that is paid out prior to any dividends to common stock holders.

a. Follow-on offering
b. Second lien loan
c. Trade-off theory
d. Preferred stock

13. In accounting, _________ refers to the portion of net income which is retained by the corporation rather than distributed to its owners as dividends. Similarly, if the corporation makes a loss, then that loss is retained and called variously retained losses, accumulated losses or accumulated deficit. _________ and losses are cumulative from year to year with losses offsetting earnings.

a. Matching principle
b. Historical cost
c. Generally Accepted Accounting Principles
d. Retained earnings

14. _________ is a form of corporation equity ownership represented in the securities. It is dangerous in comparison to preferred shares and some other investment options, in that in the event of bankruptcy, _________ investors receive their funds after preferred stockholders, bondholders, creditors, etc. On the other hand, common shares on average perform better than preferred shares or bonds over time.
a. Stock market bubble
b. Stop-limit order
c. Stock split
d. Common stock

15. The _________ is the rate that a company is expected to pay to finance its assets. WACC is the minimum return that a company must earn on existing asset base to satisfy its creditors, owners, and other providers of capital.

Companies raise money from a number of sources: common equity, preferred equity, straight debt, convertible debt, exchangeable debt, warrants, options, pension liabilities, executive stock options, governmental subsidies, and so on.

a. Cost of capital
b. Weighted average cost of capital
c. 4-4-5 Calendar
d. Capital intensity

16. The _________ is an expected return that the provider of capital plans to earn on their investment.

Capital (money) used for funding a business should earn returns for the capital providers who risk their capital. For an investment to be worthwhile, the expected return on capital must be greater than the _________.

a. 4-4-5 Calendar
b. Weighted average cost of capital
c. Cost of capital
d. Capital intensity

17. In economics and finance, _________ is the change in total cost that arises when the quantity produced changes by one unit. It is the cost of producing one more unit of a good. Mathematically, the _________ function is expressed as the first derivative of the total cost (TC) function with respect to quantity (Q). Note that the _________ may change with volume, and so at each level of production, the _________ is the cost of the next unit produced.

A typical _________ Curve

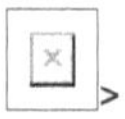
>

a. Marginal cost
b. Sliding scale fees
c. Cost accounting
d. Fixed costs

18. In options, the _________ is a key variable in a derivatives contract between two parties. Where the contract requires delivery of the underlying instrument, the trade will be at the _________, regardless of the spot price (market price) of the underlying instrument at that time.

Definition - The fixed price at which the owner of an option can purchase, in the case of a call in the case of a put, the underlying security or commodity.

a. Swaption
b. Strike price
c. Moneyness
d. Naked put

1. In business and accounting, _________s are everything of value that is owned by a person or company. The balance sheet of a firm records the monetary value of the _________s owned by the firm. The two major _________ classes are tangible _________s and intangible _________s.

a. Asset
b. Accounts payable
c. EBITDA
d. Income

2. In finance, _________ is the process of estimating the potential market value of a financial asset or liability. they can be done on assets (for example, investments in marketable securities such as stocks, options, business enterprises, or intangible assets such as patents and trademarks) or on liabilities (e.g., Bonds issued by a company.) _________s are required in many contexts including investment analysis, capital budgeting, merger and acquisition transactions, financial reporting, taxable events to determine the proper tax liability, and in litigation.

a. Share
b. Procter ' Gamble
c. Margin
d. Valuation

3. In finance, _________, also known as return on investment is the ratio of money gained or lost on an investment relative to the amount of money invested. The amount of money gained or lost may be referred to as interest, profit/loss, gain/loss, or net income/loss. The money invested may be referred to as the asset, capital, principal, or the cost basis of the investment.

a. Rate of return
b. Doctrine of the Proper Law
c. Composiition of Creditors
d. Stock or scrip dividends

4. _________ is the balance of the amounts of cash being received and paid by a business during a defined period of time, sometimes tied to a specific project. Measurement of _________ can be used

- to evaluate the state or performance of a business or project.
- to determine problems with liquidity. Being profitable does not necessarily mean being liquid. A company can fail because of a shortage of cash, even while profitable.
- to generate project rate of returns. The time of _________s into and out of projects are used as inputs to financial models such as internal rate of return, and net present value.
- to examine income or growth of a business when it is believed that accrual accounting concepts do not represent economic realities. Alternately, _________ can be used to 'validate' the net income generated by accrual accounting.

_________ as a generic term may be used differently depending on context, and certain _________ definitions may be adapted by analysts and users for their own uses. Common terms include operating _________ and free _________.

_________s can be classified into:

1. Operational _________s: Cash received or expended as a result of the company's core business activities.
2. Investment _________s: Cash received or expended through capital expenditure, investments or acquisitions.
3. Financing _________s: Cash received or expended as a result of financial activities, such as interests and dividends.

All three together - the net _________ - are necessary to reconcile the beginning cash balance to the ending cash balance. Loan draw downs or equity injections, that is just shifting of capital but no expenditure as such, are not considered in the net _________.

a. Real option
b. Corporate finance
c. Shareholder value
d. Cash flow

5. _________, refers to consumption opportunity gained by an entity within a specified time frame, which is generally expressed in monetary terms. However, for households and individuals, '_________ is the sum of all the wages, salaries, profits, interests payments, rents and other forms of earnings received... in a given period of time.' For firms, _________ generally refers to net-profit: what remains of revenue after expenses have been subtracted.
a. Annual report
b. OIBDA
c. Accrual
d. Income

6. In economics, an _________ or spillover of an economic transaction is an impact on a party that is not directly involved in the transaction. In such a case, prices do not reflect the full costs or benefits in production or consumption of a product or service. A positive impact is called an external benefit, while a negative impact is called an external cost.
a. AAB
b. ABN Amro
c. A Random Walk Down Wall Street
d. Externality

7. In economics, business, and accounting, a _________ is the value of money that has been used up to produce something, and hence is not available for use anymore. In business, the _________ may be one of acquisition, in which case the amount of money expended to acquire it is counted as _________. In this case, money is the input that is gone in order to acquire the thing.

a. Fixed costs
b. Sliding scale fees
c. Marginal cost
d. Cost

8. In financial accounting, _________ , cash flow provided by operations or cash flow from operating activities, refers to the amount of cash a company generates from the revenues it brings in, excluding costs associated with long-term investment on capital items or investment in securities.

_________ = Cash generated from operations less taxation and interest paid, investment income received and less dividends paid gives rise to _________s per International Financial Reporting Standards.

To calculate cash generated from operations, one must calculate cash generated from customers and cash paid to suppliers.

a. Appreciation
b. A Random Walk Down Wall Street
c. Other Comprehensive Basis of Accounting
d. Operating cash flow

9. The _________ is a capital budgeting metric used by firms to decide whether they should make investments. It is an indicator of the efficiency or quality of an investment, as opposed to net present value (NPV), which indicates value or magnitude.

The IRR is the annualized effective compounded return rate which can be earned on the invested capital, i.e., the yield on the investment.

a. A Random Walk Down Wall Street
b. Internal rate of return
c. ABN Amro
d. AAB

10. _________ is equal to the income that a firm has after subtracting costs and expenses from the total revenue. _________ can be distributed among holders of common stock as a dividend or held by the firm as retained earnings. _________ is an accounting term; in some countries (such as the UK) profit is the usual term.

a. Historical cost
b. Furniture, Fixtures and Equipment
c. Net income
d. Write-off

11. _________ or net present worth (NPW) is defined as the total present value (PV) of a time series of cash flows. It is a standard method for using the time value of money to appraise long-term projects. Used for capital budgeting, and widely throughout economics, it measures the excess or shortfall of cash flows, in present value terms, once financing charges are met.

a. Present value of costs
b. Tax shield
c. Negative gearing
d. Net present value

12. _________ is the difference between operating revenues and operating expenses, but it is also sometimes used as a synonym for EBIT and operating profit. This is true if the firm has no non-_________.

A professional investor contemplating a change to the capital structure of a firm (e.g., through a leveraged buyout) first evaluates a firm's fundamental earnings potential (reflected by Earnings Before Interest, Taxes, Depreciation and Amortization EBITDA and EBIT), and then determines the optimal use of debt vs. equity.

a. Operating income
b. A Random Walk Down Wall Street
c. ABN Amro
d. AAB

13. _________ is the value on a given date of a future payment or series of future payments, discounted to reflect the time value of money and other factors such as investment risk. _________ calculations are widely used in business and economics to provide a means to compare cash flows at different times on a meaningful 'like to like' basis.

The most commonly applied model of the time value of money is compound interest.

a. Present value of benefits
b. Negative gearing
c. Net present value
d. Present value

14. A mutual shareholder or _________ is an individual or company (including a corporation) that legally owns one or more shares of stock in a joint stock company. A company's shareholders collectively own that company. Thus, the typical goal of such companies is to enhance shareholder value.

a. Stockholder
b. Limit order
c. Trading curb
d. Stock market bubble

15. _________ is the planning process used to determine whether a firm's long term investments such as new machinery, replacement machinery, new plants, new products, and research development projects are worth pursuing. It is budget for major capital, or investment, expenditures.

Many formal methods are used in _________, including the techniques such as

- Net present value
- Profitability index
- Internal rate of return
- Modified Internal Rate of Return
- Equivalent annuity

These methods use the incremental cash flows from each potential investment, or project. Techniques based on accounting earnings and accounting rules are sometimes used - though economists consider this to be improper - such as the accounting rate of return, and 'return on investment.' Simplified and hybrid methods are used as well, such as payback period and discounted payback period.

a. Capital budgeting
b. Shareholder value
c. Preferred stock
d. Financial distress

16. _________ refers to a business or organization attempting to acquire goods or services to accomplish the goals of the enterprise. Though there are several organizations that attempt to set standards in the _________ process, processes can vary greatly between organizations. Typically the word '_________' is not used interchangeably with the word 'procurement', since procurement typically includes Expediting, Supplier Quality, and Traffic and Logistics (T'L) in addition to _________.

a. Purchasing
b. 4-4-5 Calendar
c. 529 plan
d. 7-Eleven

17. _________ is the value of goods/services compared to the amount paid with a currency. Currency can be either a commodity money, like gold or silver, or fiat currency like US dollars which are the world reserve currency. As Adam Smith noted, having money gives one the ability to 'command' others' labor, so _________ to some extent is power over other people, to the extent that they are willing to trade their labor or goods for money or currency.

a. 7-Eleven
b. 4-4-5 Calendar
c. 529 plan
d. Purchasing power

18. In finance, a _________ is a debt security, in which the authorized issuer owes the holders a debt and, depending on the terms of the _________, is obliged to pay interest (the coupon) and/or to repay the principal at a later date, termed maturity.

Thus a _________ is a loan: the issuer is the borrower, the _________ holder is the lender, and the coupon is the interest. _________s provide the borrower with external funds to finance long-term investments, or, in the case of government _________s, to finance current expenditure.

a. Convertible bond
b. Catastrophe bonds
c. Puttable bond
d. Bond

19. A '_________' is a 'Charge' that is paid to obtain the right to delay a payment. Essentially, the payer purchases the right to make a given payment in the future instead of in the Present. The '_________', or 'Charge' that must be paid to delay the payment, is simply the difference between what the payment amount would be if it were paid in the present and what the payment amount would be paid if it were paid in the future.

a. Discount
b. Risk aversion
c. Risk modeling
d. Value at risk

20. The _________ is an interest rate a central bank charges depository institutions that borrow reserves from it.

The term _________ has two meanings:

- the same as interest rate; the term 'discount' does not refer to the meaning of the word, but to the purpose of using the quantity, such as computations of present value, e.g. net present value / discounted cash flow

- the annual effective _________, which is the annual interest divided by the capital including that interest; this rate is lower than the interest rate; it corresponds to using the value after a year as the nominal value, and seeing the initial value as the nominal value minus a discount; it is used for Treasury Bills and similar financial instruments

The annual effective _________ is the annual interest divided by the capital including that interest, which is the interest rate divided by 100% plus the interest rate. It is the annual discount factor to be applied to the future cash flow, to find the discount, subtracted from a future value to find the value one year earlier.

For example, suppose there is a government bond that sells for $95 and pays $100 in a year's time.

a. Stochastic volatility
b. Discount rate
c. Fisher equation
d. Black-Scholes

21. When foreign currency is converted back to the currency of the home country it is referred to as _________. An example would be an American converting British Pounds back to U.S. Dollars.

_________ also refers to the payment of a dividend by a foreign corporation to a US corporation. This happens often where the foreign corporation is considered a 'controlled foreign corporation' , which means that it more than 50% of the foreign corporation is owned by US shareholders.

a. Anton Gelonkin
b. Andrew Tobias
c. Adolph Coors
d. Repatriation

22. In finance, the _________ between two currencies specifies how much one currency is worth in terms of the other. For example an _________ of 102 Japanese yen to the United States dollar means that JPY 102 is worth the same as USD 1. The foreign exchange market is one of the largest markets in the world.

a. A Random Walk Down Wall Street
b. ABN Amro
c. AAB
d. Exchange rate

23. _________ is a form of risk that arises from the change in price of one currency against another. Whenever investors or companies have assets or business operations across national borders, they face _________ if their positions are not hedged.

- Transaction risk is the risk that exchange rates will change unfavourably over time. It can be hedged against using forward currency contracts;
- Translation risk is an accounting risk, proportional to the amount of assets held in foreign currencies. Changes in the exchange rate over time will render a report inaccurate, and so assets are usually balanced by borrowings in that currency.

The exchange risk associated with a foreign denominated instrument is a key element in foreign investment. This risk flows from differential monetary policy and growth in real productivity, which results in differential inflation rates.

a. Market risk
b. Credit risk
c. Tracking error
d. Currency risk

24. _________ is a type of risk faced by investors, corporations, and governments. It is a risk that can be understood and managed with proper aforethought and investment.

Broadly, _________ refers to the complications businesses and governments may face as a result of what are commonly referred to as political decisions--or 'any political change that alters the expected outcome and value of a given economic action by changing the probability of achieving business objectives.' .

a. Capital asset
b. Mid price
c. Single-index model
d. Political risk

25. _________ is a term used in accounting, economics and finance to spread the cost of an asset over the span of several years.

In simple words we can say that _________ is the reduction in the value of an asset due to usage, passage of time, wear and tear, technological outdating or obsolescence, depletion or other such factors.

In accounting, _________ is a term used to describe any method of attributing the historical or purchase cost of an asset across its useful life, roughly corresponding to normal wear and tear.

a. Bottom line
b. Depreciation
c. Deferred financing costs
d. Matching principle

26. Accrual, in accounting, describes the accounting method known as _________, whereby revenues and expenses are recognized when they are accrued, i.e. accumulated (earned or incurred), regardless when the actual cash is received or paid out.

E.g. a company delivers a product to a customer who will pay for it 30 days later in the next fiscal year starting a week after the delivery. The company recognizes the proceeds as a revenue in its current income statement still for the fiscal year of the delivery, even though it will get paid in cash during the following accounting period.

a. ABN Amro
b. Accrual basis
c. A Random Walk Down Wall Street
d. AAB

1. The institution most often referenced by the word '_________' is a public or publicly traded _________, the shares of which are traded on a public stock exchange (e.g., the New York Stock Exchange or Nasdaq in the United States) where shares of stock of _________s are bought and sold by and to the general public. Most of the largest businesses in the world are publicly traded _________s. However, the majority of _________s are said to be closely held, privately held or close _________s, meaning that no ready market exists for the trading of shares.

a. Depository Trust Company
b. Protect
c. Federal Home Loan Mortgage Corporation
d. Corporation

2. _________ is that which is owed; usually referencing assets owed, but the term can cover other obligations. In the case of assets, _________ is a means of using future purchasing power in the present before a summation has been earned. Some companies and corporations use _________ as a part of their overall corporate finance strategy.

a. Credit cycle
b. Partial Payment
c. Cross-collateralization
d. Debt

3. In business and accounting, _________s are everything of value that is owned by a person or company. The balance sheet of a firm records the monetary value of the _________s owned by the firm. The two major _________ classes are tangible _________s and intangible _________s.

a. Accounts payable
b. Income
c. EBITDA
d. Asset

4. A _________ is a payment made by a corporation to its shareholder members. When a corporation earns a profit or surplus, that money can be put to two uses: it can either be re-invested in the business (called retained earnings), or it can be paid to the shareholders as a _________. Many corporations retain a portion of their earnings and pay the remainder as a _________.

a. Dividend
b. Special dividend
c. Dividend yield
d. Dividend puzzle

5. In finance, _________ is the process of estimating the potential market value of a financial asset or liability. they can be done on assets (for example, investments in marketable securities such as stocks, options, business enterprises, or intangible assets such as patents and trademarks) or on liabilities (e.g., Bonds issued by a company.) _________s are required in many contexts including investment analysis, capital budgeting, merger and acquisition transactions, financial reporting, taxable events to determine the proper tax liability, and in litigation.
   a. Margin
   b. Share
   c. Valuation
   d. Procter ' Gamble

6. In finance, _________ (or gearing) is borrowing money to supplement existing funds for investment in such a way that the potential positive or negative outcome is magnified and/or enhanced. It generally refers to using borrowed funds, or debt, so as to attempt to increase the returns to equity. Deleveraging is the action of reducing borrowings.
   a. Financial endowment
   b. Limited partnership
   c. Pension fund
   d. Leverage

7. In finance, _________ refers to the way a corporation finances its assets through some combination of equity, debt, or hybrid securities. A firm's _________ is then the composition or 'structure' of its liabilities. For example, a firm that sells $20 billion in equity and $80 billion in debt is said to be 20% equity-financed and 80% debt-financed.
   a. Rights issue
   b. Market for corporate control
   c. Book building
   d. Capital structure

8. In economics, business, and accounting, a _________ is the value of money that has been used up to produce something, and hence is not available for use anymore. In business, the _________ may be one of acquisition, in which case the amount of money expended to acquire it is counted as _________. In this case, money is the input that is gone in order to acquire the thing.
   a. Marginal cost
   b. Fixed costs
   c. Cost
   d. Sliding scale fees

9. The _________ is an expected return that the provider of capital plans to earn on their investment.

Capital (money) used for funding a business should earn returns for the capital providers who risk their capital. For an investment to be worthwhile, the expected return on capital must be greater than the _________.

a. Weighted average cost of capital
b. 4-4-5 Calendar
c. Capital intensity
d. Cost of capital

10. A _________ is the price of a single share of a no. of saleable stocks of the company. Once the stock is purchased, the owner becomes a shareholder of the company that issued the share.

a. Whisper numbers
b. Stock split
c. Trading curb
d. Share price

11. _________ is a measure of the ability of a debtor to pay their debts as and when they fall due. It is usually expressed as a ratio or a percentage of current liabilities.

For a corporation with a published balance sheet there are various ratios used to calculate a measure of liquidity.

a. Operating leverage
b. Operating profit margin
c. Invested capital
d. Accounting liquidity

12. A _________ is a situation that involves losing one quality or aspect of something in return for gaining another quality or aspect. It implies a decision to be made with full comprehension of both the upside and downside of a particular choice.

In economics the term is expressed as opportunity cost, referring the most preferred alternative given up.

a. Total revenue
b. Capital outflow
c. Break-even point
d. Trade-off

13. In economics and contract theory, _________ deals with the study of decisions in transactions where one party has more or better information than the other. This creates an imbalance of power in transactions which can sometimes cause the transactions to go awry. Examples of this problem are adverse selection and moral hazard.

a. AAB
b. A Random Walk Down Wall Street
c. ABN Amro
d. Information asymmetry

14. _________ and the related Fisher's linear discriminant are methods used in statistics and machine learning to find the linear combination of features which best separate two or more classes of objects or events. The resulting combination may be used as a linear classifier, or, more commonly, for dimensionality reduction before later classification.

_________ is closely related to ANOVA (analysis of variance) and regression analysis, which also attempt to express one dependent variable as a linear combination of other features or measurements.

a. Linear discriminant analysis
b. 529 plan
c. 4-4-5 Calendar
d. 7-Eleven

15. _________ represents the impact on the stock price that investors would cause in reaction to a change in policy of a company.

a. Bonus share
b. Clientele effect
c. Volatility clustering
d. Trade date

16. In corporate finance, _________ is a cash flow available for distribution among all the security holders of a company. They include equity holders, debt holders, preferred stock holders, convertible security holders, and so on.

Note that the first three lines above are calculated for you on the standard Statement of Cash Flows.

a. Funding
b. Forfaiting
c. Safety stock
d. Free cash flow

17. _________ is the balance of the amounts of cash being received and paid by a business during a defined period of time, sometimes tied to a specific project. Measurement of _________ can be used

- to evaluate the state or performance of a business or project.
- to determine problems with liquidity. Being profitable does not necessarily mean being liquid. A company can fail because of a shortage of cash, even while profitable.
- to generate project rate of returns. The time of _________s into and out of projects are used as inputs to financial models such as internal rate of return, and net present value.
- to examine income or growth of a business when it is believed that accrual accounting concepts do not represent economic realities. Alternately, _________ can be used to 'validate' the net income generated by accrual accounting.

_________ as a generic term may be used differently depending on context, and certain _________ definitions may be adapted by analysts and users for their own uses. Common terms include operating _________ and free _________.

_________s can be classified into:

1. Operational _________s: Cash received or expended as a result of the company's core business activities.
2. Investment _________s: Cash received or expended through capital expenditure, investments or acquisitions.
3. Financing _________s: Cash received or expended as a result of financial activities, such as interests and dividends.

All three together - the net _________ - are necessary to reconcile the beginning cash balance to the ending cash balance. Loan draw downs or equity injections, that is just shifting of capital but no expenditure as such, are not considered in the net _________.

a. Corporate finance
b. Shareholder value
c. Cash flow
d. Real option

18. _________ is the fraction of net income a firm pays to its stockholders in dividends:

The part of the earnings not paid to investors is left for investment to provide for future earnings growth. Investors seeking high current income and limited capital growth prefer companies with high _________. However investors seeking capital growth may prefer lower payout ratio because capital gains are taxed at a lower rate.

a. Dividend imputation
b. Dividend payout ratio
c. Dividend yield
d. Dividend puzzle

19. The key date to remember for dividend paying stocks is the _________. The _________ is different from the record date. The _________ is typically two trading days before the record date.

In order to receive the upcoming dividend payment payout, you must already own or you must purchase the stock prior to the _________. It is important to note that in most countries, when you buy or sell any stock, there is a three trading-day settlement period on your order.

a. Ex-dividend date
b. Asian Financial Crisis
c. Index number
d. Insolvency

20. A _________ or stock divide increases or decreases the number of shares in a public company. The price is adjusted such that the before and after market capitalization of the company remains the same and dilution does not occur. Options and warrants are included.
a. Contract for difference
b. Stop price
c. Stop order
d. Stock split

21. _________ are those dividends paid out in form of additional stock shares of the issuing corporation or other corporation They are usually issued in proportion to shares owned (for example for every 100 shares of stock owned, 5% stock dividend will yield 5 extra shares). If this payment involves the issue of new shares, this is very similar to a stock split in that it increases the total number of shares while lowering the price of each share and does not change the market capitalization or the total value of the shares held
a. Time-based currency
b. Database auditing
c. The Hong Kong Securities Institute
d. Stock or scrip dividends

22. In financial accounting, a _________ or statement of financial position is a summary of a person's or organization's balances. Assets, liabilities and ownership equity are listed as of a specific date, such as the end of its financial year. A _________ is often described as a snapshot of a company's financial condition.

a. Statement on Auditing Standards No. 70: Service Organizations
b. Statement of retained earnings
c. Balance sheet
d. Financial statements

1. _________ is a legally declared inability or impairment of ability of an individual or organization to pay their creditors. Creditors may file a _________ petition against a debtor ('involuntary _________') in an effort to recoup a portion of what they are owed or initiate a restructuring. In the majority of cases, however, _________ is initiated by the debtor (a 'voluntary _________' that is filed by the bankrupt individual or organization.)

a. 4-4-5 Calendar
b. 529 plan
c. Bankruptcy
d. Debt settlement

2. _________ is a financial metric which represents operating liquidity available to a business. Along with fixed assets such as plant and equipment, _________ is considered a part of operating capital. It is calculated as current assets minus current liabilities.

a. 4-4-5 Calendar
b. Working capital management
c. Working capital
d. 529 plan

3. _________ or financing is to provide capital (funds), which means money for a project, a person, a business or any other private or public institutions.

Those funds can be allocated for either short term or long term purposes. The health fund is a new way of _________ private healthcare centers.

a. Synthetic CDO
b. Product life cycle
c. Proxy fight
d. Funding

4. In business and accounting, _________s are everything of value that is owned by a person or company. The balance sheet of a firm records the monetary value of the _________s owned by the firm. The two major _________ classes are tangible _________s and intangible _________s.

a. Income
b. Accounts payable
c. EBITDA
d. Asset

5. In accounting, a _________ is an asset on the balance sheet which is expected to be sold or otherwise used up in the near future, usually within one year, or one business cycle - whichever is longer. Typical _________s include cash, cash equivalents, accounts receivable, inventory, the portion of prepaid accounts which will be used within a year, and short-term investments.

On the balance sheet, assets will typically be classified into _________s and long-term assets.

a. Write-off
b. Long-term liabilities
c. Current asset
d. Historical cost

6. An _________ is any government regulation or law that encourages or discourages foreign investment in the local economy, e.g. currency exchange limits.

As globalization integrates the economies of neighboring and of trading states, they are typically forced to trade off such rules as part of a common tax, tariff and trade regime, e.g. as defined by a free trade pact. _________ favoring local investors over global ones is typically discouraged in such pacts, and the idea of a separate _________ rapidly becomes a fiction or fantasy, as real decisions reflect the real need for nations to compete for investment, even from their own local investors.

a. A Random Walk Down Wall Street
b. AAB
c. ABN Amro
d. Investment policy

7. _________ is a life of security. It may also refer to the final payment date of a loan or other financial instrument, at which point all remaining interest and principal is due to be paid.

1, 3, 6 months _________ band can be calculated by using 30-day per month periods.

a. Primary market
b. False billing
c. Maturity
d. Replacement cost

8. _________ exists when one firm provides goods or services to a customer with an agreement to bill them later, or receive a shipment or service from a supplier under an agreement to pay them later. It can be viewed as an essential element of capitalization in an operating business because it can reduce the required capital investment to operate the business if it is managed properly. _________ is the largest use of capital for a majority of business to business (B2B) sellers in the United States and is a critical source of capital for a majority of all businesses.

a. Trade credit
b. 4-4-5 Calendar
c. Going concern
d. 529 plan

9. _________ is the provision of resources (such as granting a loan) by one party to another party where that second party does not reimburse the first party immediately, thereby generating a debt, and instead arranges either to repay or return those resources (or material(s) of equal value) at a later date. The first party is called a creditor, also known as a lender, while the second party is called a debtor, also known as a borrower.

Movements of financial capital are normally dependent on either _________ or equity transfers.

a. Comparable
b. Credit
c. Warrant
d. Clearing house

10. A _________ is any credit facility extended to a business by a bank or financial institution. A _________ may take several forms such as cash credit, overdraft, demand loan, export packing credit, term loan, discounting or purchase of commercial bills etc. It is like an account that can readily be tapped into if the need arises or not touched at all and saved for emergencies.

a. Line of credit
b. Default Notice
c. Cash credit
d. Debt-snowball method

11. A _________, referred to as a note payable in accounting, is a contract where one party (the maker or issuer) makes an unconditional promise in writing to pay a sum of money to the other (the payee), either at a fixed or determinable future time or on demand of the payee, under specific terms. They differ from IOUs in that they contain a specific promise to pay, rather than simply acknowledging that a debt exists.

The terms of a note typically include the principal amount, the interest rate if any, and the maturity date.

a. Financial plan
b. Title loan
c. Credit repair software
d. Promissory note

12. _________ is a financial transaction whereby a business sells its accounts receivable (i.e., invoices) at a discount. _________ differs from a bank loan in three main ways. First, the emphasis is on the value of the receivables (essentially a financial asset), not the firm's credit worthiness.

a. Financial Literacy Month
b. Debt-for-equity swap
c. Credit card balance transfer
d. Factoring

13. In economics, business, and accounting, a _________ is the value of money that has been used up to produce something, and hence is not available for use anymore. In business, the _________ may be one of acquisition, in which case the amount of money expended to acquire it is counted as _________. In this case, money is the input that is gone in order to acquire the thing.

a. Marginal cost
b. Fixed costs
c. Sliding scale fees
d. Cost

14. In economics, the concept of the _________ refers to the decision-making time frame of a firm in which at least one factor of production is fixed. Costs which are fixed in the _________ have no impact on a firms decisions. For example a firm can raise output by increasing the amount of labour through overtime.

a. 4-4-5 Calendar
b. 529 plan
c. Long-run
d. Short-run

15. _________ is a fee paid on borrowed assets. It is the price paid for the use of borrowed money , or, money earned by deposited funds . Assets that are sometimes lent with _________ include money, shares, consumer goods through hire purchase, major assets such as aircraft, and even entire factories in finance lease arrangements.

a. AAB
b. Insolvency
c. Interest
d. A Random Walk Down Wall Street

16. _________ are securities that can be easily converted into cash. Such securities will generally have highly liquid markets allowing the security to be sold at a reasonable price very quickly.This is a usual feature in real estate .
a. Book entry
b. Securities lending
c. Tracking stock
d. Marketable

17. A _________ is a fungible, negotiable instrument representing financial value. They are broadly categorized into debt securities (such as banknotes, bonds and debentures), and equity securities; e.g., common stocks. The company or other entity issuing the _________ is called the issuer.
a. Securities lending
b. Security
c. Tracking stock
d. Book entry

18. _________, in bookkeeping, refers to assets, liabilities, income, and expenses recorded on individual pages of the so called book of final entry or ledger. Changes in _________ value are made by chronologically posting debit (DR) and credit (CR) entries to its page. Examples of _________s are cash, _________s receivable, mortgages, loans, land and buildings, common stock, sales, services provided, wages, and payroll overhead.
a. Accretion
b. Account
c. Alpha
d. Option

19. _________ is the balance of the amounts of cash being received and paid by a business during a defined period of time, sometimes tied to a specific project. Measurement of _________ can be used

- to evaluate the state or performance of a business or project.
- to determine problems with liquidity. Being profitable does not necessarily mean being liquid. A company can fail because of a shortage of cash, even while profitable.
- to generate project rate of returns. The time of _________s into and out of projects are used as inputs to financial models such as internal rate of return, and net present value.
- to examine income or growth of a business when it is believed that accrual accounting concepts do not represent economic realities. Alternately, _________ can be used to 'validate' the net income generated by accrual accounting.

_________ as a generic term may be used differently depending on context, and certain _________ definitions may be adapted by analysts and users for their own uses. Common terms include operating _________ and free _________.

_________s can be classified into:

1. Operational _________s: Cash received or expended as a result of the company's core business activities.
2. Investment _________s: Cash received or expended through capital expenditure, investments or acquisitions.
3. Financing _________s: Cash received or expended as a result of financial activities, such as interests and dividends.

All three together - the net _________ - are necessary to reconcile the beginning cash balance to the ending cash balance. Loan draw downs or equity injections, that is just shifting of capital but no expenditure as such, are not considered in the net _________.

a. Shareholder value
b. Cash flow
c. Corporate finance
d. Real option

20. In United States banking, _________ is a marketing term for certain services offered primarily to larger business customers. It may be used to describe all bank accounts (such as checking accounts) provided to businesses of a certain size, but it is more often used to describe specific services such as cash concentration, zero balance accounting, and automated clearing house facilities. Sometimes, private banking customers are given _________ services.

a. Profitability index
b. Global tactical asset allocation
c. Cash management
d. Capitalization rate

21. The free _________ of a public company is an estimate of the proportion of shares that are not held by large owners and that are not stock with sales restrictions (restricted stock that cannot be sold until they become unrestricted stock.)

The free _________ or a public _________ is usually defined as being all shares held by investors other than:

- shares held by owners owning more than 5% of all shares (those could be institutional investors, 'strategic shareholders,' founders, executives, and other insiders' holdings)
- restricted stocks (granted to executives that can be, but don't have to be, registered insiders)
- insider holdings (it is assumed that insiders hold stock for the very long term)

The free _________ is an important criterion in quoting a share on the stock market.

To _________ a company means to list its shares on a public stock exchange through an initial public offering (or 'flotation'.)

- Open market
- Outstanding shares
- Market capitalization
- Public _________ *loat*
- Reverse takeover

.

a. Trade finance
b. Synthetic CDO
c. Float
d. Golden parachute

22. A '_________' is a 'Charge' that is paid to obtain the right to delay a payment. Essentially, the payer purchases the right to make a given payment in the future instead of in the Present. The '_________', or 'Charge' that must be paid to delay the payment, is simply the difference between what the payment amount would be if it were paid in the present and what the payment amount would be paid if it were paid in the future.
a. Value at risk
b. Risk modeling
c. Risk aversion
d. Discount

23. In finance, _________ is the process of estimating the potential market value of a financial asset or liability. they can be done on assets (for example, investments in marketable securities such as stocks, options, business enterprises, or intangible assets such as patents and trademarks) or on liabilities (e.g., Bonds issued by a company.) _________s are required in many contexts including investment analysis, capital budgeting, merger and acquisition transactions, financial reporting, taxable events to determine the proper tax liability, and in litigation.

a. Valuation
b. Margin
c. Share
d. Procter ' Gamble

24. _________s are goods that have completed the manufacturing process but have not yet been sold or distributed to the end user.

Manufacturing has three classes of inventory:

1. Raw material
2. Work in process
3. _________s

A good purchased as a 'raw material' goes into the manufacture of a product. A good only partially completed during the manufacturing process is called 'work in process'. When the good is completed as to manufacturing but not yet sold or distributed to the end-user is called a '_________'.

a. Finished good
b. 529 plan
c. 4-4-5 Calendar
d. 7-Eleven

25. _________ is a list for goods and materials held available in stock by a business. It is also used for a list of the contents of a household and for a list for testamentary purposes of the possessions of someone who has died. In accounting _________ is considered an asset.
a. Inventory
b. ABN Amro
c. A Random Walk Down Wall Street
d. AAB

26. _________ refers to government attempts to influence the direction of the economy through changes in government taxes, or through some spending (fiscal allowances.)

_________ can be contrasted with the other main type of economic policy, monetary policy, which attempts to stabilize the economy by controlling interest rates and the supply of money. The two main instruments of _________ are government spending and taxation.

a. Tax exemption
b. Tax incidence
c. Qualified residence interest
d. Fiscal policy

27. The _________ is the level of inventory when a fresh order should be made with suppliers to bring the inventory up by the Economic order quantity ('EOQ'.)

The _________ for replenishment of stock occurs when the level of inventory drops down to zero. In view of instantaneous replenishment of stock the level of inventory jumps to the original level from zero level.

a. Reorder point
b. 7-Eleven
c. 529 plan
d. 4-4-5 Calendar

28. _________ is a term used by inventory specialists to describe a level of extra stock that is maintained below the cycle stock to buffer against stockouts. _________ exists to counter uncertainties in supply and demand. _________ is defined as extra units of inventory carried as protection against possible stockouts .(shortfall in raw material or packaging.)

a. Funding
b. Counting house
c. Golden parachute
d. Safety stock

29. In business and finance, a _________ (also referred to as equity _________) of stock means a _________ of ownership in a corporation (company.) In the plural, stocks is often used as a synonym for _________s especially in the United States, but it is less commonly used that way outside of North America.

In the United Kingdom, South Africa, and Australia, stock can also refer to completely different financial instruments such as government bonds or, less commonly, to all kinds of marketable securities.

a. Procter ' Gamble
b. Share
c. Bucket shop
d. Margin

30. _________ is an inventory strategy implemented to improve the return on investment of a business by reducing in-process inventory and its associated carrying costs. In order to achieve _________ the process must have signals of what is going on elsewhere within the process. This means that the process is often driven by a series of signals, which can be Kanban, that tell production processes when to make the next part.

a. Debtor-in-possession financing
b. Pac-Man defense
c. Greed and fear
d. Just-in-time

31. _________ is subcontracting a process, such as product design or manufacturing, to a third-party company. The decision to outsource is often made in the interest of lowering cost or making better use of time and energy costs, redirecting or conserving energy directed at the competencies of a particular business, or to make more efficient use of land, labor, capital, (information) technology and resources. _________ became part of the business lexicon during the 1980s.

a. OTC Bulletin Board
b. Exchange Rate Mechanism
c. AT'T Inc.
d. Outsourcing

32. Decisions relating to working capital and short term financing are referred to as _________. These involve managing the relationship between a firm's short-term assets and its short-term liabilities. The goal of _________ is to ensure that the firm is able to continue its operations and that it has sufficient cash flow to satisfy both maturing short-term debt and upcoming operational expenses.

a. Working capital
b. Working capital management
c. 529 plan
d. 4-4-5 Calendar

1. A _________ is a pool of assets forming an independent legal entity that are bought with the contributions to a pension plan for the exclusive purpose of financing pension plan benefits.

_________s are important shareholders of listed and private companies. They are especially important to the stock market where large institutional investors like the Ontario Teachers' Pension Plan dominate.

a. Leveraged buyout
b. Pension fund
c. Leverage
d. Limited liability company

2. In economics, business, and accounting, a _________ is the value of money that has been used up to produce something, and hence is not available for use anymore. In business, the _________ may be one of acquisition, in which case the amount of money expended to acquire it is counted as _________. In this case, money is the input that is gone in order to acquire the thing.

a. Marginal cost
b. Cost
c. Sliding scale fees
d. Fixed costs

3. In economics and finance, _________ represents passive holdings of securities such as foreign stocks, bonds, or other financial assets, none of which entails active management or control of the securities' issuer by the investor; where such control exists, it is known as foreign direct investment. Generally, this means the investor holds less than 10% of the total shares or less than the amount needed to hold the majority vote.

Some examples of _________ are:

- purchase of shares in a foreign company.
- purchase of bonds issued by a foreign government.
- acquisition of assets in a foreign country.

Factors affecting international _________:

- tax rates on interest or dividends (investors will normally prefer countries where the tax rates are relatively low)
- interest rates (money tends to flow to countries with high interest rates)
- exchange rates (foreign investors may be attracted if the local currency is expected to strengthen)

_________ is part of the capital account on the balance of payments statistics.

a. Tactical asset allocation
b. Divestment
c. Portable alpha
d. Portfolio Investment

4. _________ is the balance of the amounts of cash being received and paid by a business during a defined period of time, sometimes tied to a specific project. Measurement of _________ can be used

- to evaluate the state or performance of a business or project.
- to determine problems with liquidity. Being profitable does not necessarily mean being liquid. A company can fail because of a shortage of cash, even while profitable.
- to generate project rate of returns. The time of _________s into and out of projects are used as inputs to financial models such as internal rate of return, and net present value.
- to examine income or growth of a business when it is believed that accrual accounting concepts do not represent economic realities. Alternately, _________ can be used to 'validate' the net income generated by accrual accounting.

_________ as a generic term may be used differently depending on context, and certain _________ definitions may be adapted by analysts and users for their own uses. Common terms include operating _________ and free _________.

_________s can be classified into:

1. Operational _________s: Cash received or expended as a result of the company's core business activities.
2. Investment _________s: Cash received or expended through capital expenditure, investments or acquisitions.
3. Financing _________s: Cash received or expended as a result of financial activities, such as interests and dividends.

All three together - the net _________ - are necessary to reconcile the beginning cash balance to the ending cash balance. Loan draw downs or equity injections, that is just shifting of capital but no expenditure as such, are not considered in the net _________.

a. Shareholder value
b. Corporate finance
c. Real option
d. Cash flow

5. _________ measures the nominal future sum of money that a given sum of money is 'worth' at a specified time in the future assuming a certain interest rate rate of return; it is the present value multiplied by the accumulation function.

The value does not include corrections for inflation or other factors that affect the true value of money in the future. This is used in time value of money calculations.

a. Future-oriented
b. Discounted cash flow
c. Future value
d. Present value of costs

6. A _________ is an institution, firm or individual who mediates between two or more parties in a financial context. Typically the first party is a provider of a product or service and the second party is a consumer or customer.

In the U.S., a _________ is typically an institution that facilitates the channelling of funds between lenders and borrowers indirectly.

a. Net asset value
b. Mutual fund
c. Financial intermediary
d. Savings and loan association

7. A _________ is a fungible, negotiable instrument representing financial value. They are broadly categorized into debt securities (such as banknotes, bonds and debentures), and equity securities; e.g., common stocks. The company or other entity issuing the _________ is called the issuer.

a. Tracking stock
b. Securities lending
c. Security
d. Book entry

8. A _________ is an order to buy a security at no more (or sell at no less) than a specific price. This gives the customer some control over the price at which the trade is executed, but may prevent the order from being executed ('filled'.)

A buy _________ can only be executed by the broker at the limit price or lower.

a. Common stock
b. Commercial mortgage-backed securities
c. Block premium
d. Limit order

9. A _________ is an order to buy (or sell) a security once the price of the security has climbed above (or dropped below) a specified stop price. When the specified stop price is reached, the _________ is entered as a market order (no limit.)

With a _________, the customer does not have to actively monitor how a stock is performing.

a. Stop order
b. Share price
c. Wash sale
d. Stock split

10. In finance, a _________ is a debt security, in which the authorized issuer owes the holders a debt and, depending on the terms of the _________, is obliged to pay interest (the coupon) and/or to repay the principal at a later date, termed maturity.

Thus a _________ is a loan: the issuer is the borrower, the _________ holder is the lender, and the coupon is the interest. _________s provide the borrower with external funds to finance long-term investments, or, in the case of government _________s, to finance current expenditure.

a. Catastrophe bonds
b. Puttable bond
c. Bond
d. Convertible bond

11. In finance, _________ is a measurement of return on an asset or portfolio. It is one of the simplest measures of investment performance.

_________ is the percentage by which the value of a portfolio (or asset) has grown for a particular period.

a. Creditor
b. Market integration
c. Stock market index option
d. Holding period return

12. _________ is the provision of resources (such as granting a loan) by one party to another party where that second party does not reimburse the first party immediately, thereby generating a debt, and instead arranges either to repay or return those resources (or material(s) of equal value) at a later date. The first party is called a creditor, also known as a lender, while the second party is called a debtor, also known as a borrower.

Movements of financial capital are normally dependent on either _________ or equity transfers.

a. Credit
b. Warrant
c. Comparable
d. Clearing house

13. In economics, the concept of the _________ refers to the decision-making time frame of a firm in which at least one factor of production is fixed. Costs which are fixed in the _________ have no impact on a firms decisions. For example a firm can raise output by increasing the amount of labour through overtime.
a. 529 plan
b. Short-run
c. 4-4-5 Calendar
d. Long-run

14. In business and accounting, _________s are everything of value that is owned by a person or company. The balance sheet of a firm records the monetary value of the _________s owned by the firm. The two major _________ classes are tangible _________s and intangible _________s.
a. EBITDA
b. Income
c. Asset
d. Accounts payable

15. In finance, _________ is the process of estimating the potential market value of a financial asset or liability. they can be done on assets (for example, investments in marketable securities such as stocks, options, business enterprises, or intangible assets such as patents and trademarks) or on liabilities (e.g., Bonds issued by a company.) _________s are required in many contexts including investment analysis, capital budgeting, merger and acquisition transactions, financial reporting, taxable events to determine the proper tax liability, and in litigation.
a. Share
b. Procter ' Gamble
c. Margin
d. Valuation

16. _________ and the related Fisher's linear discriminant are methods used in statistics and machine learning to find the linear combination of features which best separate two or more classes of objects or events. The resulting combination may be used as a linear classifier, or, more commonly, for dimensionality reduction before later classification.

_________ is closely related to ANOVA (analysis of variance) and regression analysis, which also attempt to express one dependent variable as a linear combination of other features or measurements.

a. 529 plan
b. Linear discriminant analysis
c. 4-4-5 Calendar
d. 7-Eleven

17. In finance, the term _________ describes the amount in cash that returns to the owners of a security. Normally it does not include the price variations, at the difference of the total return. _________ applies to various stated rates of return on stocks (common and preferred, and convertible), fixed income instruments (bonds, notes, bills, strips, zero coupon), and some other investment type insurance products (e.g. annuities.)

a. 4-4-5 Calendar
b. Macaulay duration
c. Yield to maturity
d. Yield

18. A _________ is the direction in which a financial market is moving. _________s can be classified as primary trends, secondary trends (short-term), and secular trends (long-term.) This principle incorporates the idea that market cycles occur with regularity and persistence.

a. 4-4-5 Calendar
b. Market trend
c. 7-Eleven
d. 529 plan

19. An _________ is an investment product other than traditional investments such as stocks, bonds or cash.

This broad definition makes it impossible to list all alternative strategies, but the most important areas are real estate, private equity, venture capital,commodities, and hedged or absolute return strategies. Wine, art and antiques, indeed any business of value, might also be considered as an _________.

a. Asset allocation
b. Investing online
c. Investment decisions
d. Alternative investment

20. Generally, in English and American law, a contract of mortgage or pledge as collateral for a debt in which the subject matter is not delivered into the possession of the pledgee or pawnee. The arrangement is common with modern mortgages - the borrower retains legal ownership of the property but provides the lender with a lien over the property until the debt is paid off.

_________ and re-_________, respectively, are commonly used to describe the means by which securities brokers and dealers first extend credit on margin to their customers using pledged securities as collateral, and then pledge the client-owned securities held in the client's margin account as collateral for the brokerage's bank loan.

a. Hypothecation
b. 529 plan
c. 7-Eleven
d. 4-4-5 Calendar

21. In finance, _________ or 'shorting' is the practice of selling a financial instrument that the seller does not own at the time of the sale. _________ is done with intent of later purchasing the financial instrument at a lower price. Short-sellers attempt to profit from an expected decline in the price of a financial instrument.
a. 529 plan
b. Short ratio
c. 4-4-5 Calendar
d. Short selling

22. In business and finance, a _________ (also referred to as equity _________) of stock means a _________ of ownership in a corporation (company.) In the plural, stocks is often used as a synonym for _________s especially in the United States, but it is less commonly used that way outside of North America.

In the United Kingdom, South Africa, and Australia, stock can also refer to completely different financial instruments such as government bonds or, less commonly, to all kinds of marketable securities.

a. Margin
b. Procter ' Gamble
c. Bucket shop
d. Share

1. A _________ is a fungible, negotiable instrument representing financial value. They are broadly categorized into debt securities (such as banknotes, bonds and debentures), and equity securities; e.g., common stocks. The company or other entity issuing the _________ is called the issuer.

a. Tracking stock
b. Securities lending
c. Book entry
d. Security

2. In business and finance, a _________ (also referred to as equity _________) of stock means a _________ of ownership in a corporation (company.) In the plural, stocks is often used as a synonym for _________s especially in the United States, but it is less commonly used that way outside of North America.

In the United Kingdom, South Africa, and Australia, stock can also refer to completely different financial instruments such as government bonds or, less commonly, to all kinds of marketable securities.

a. Share
b. Procter ' Gamble
c. Margin
d. Bucket shop

3. _________ of a business involves analyzing its financial statements and health, its management and competitive advantages, and its competitors and markets. The term is used to distinguish such analysis from other types of investment analysis, such as quantitative analysis and technical analysis.

_________ is performed on historical and present data, but with the goal of making financial forecasts.

a. Fundamental analysis
b. Stock valuation
c. 4-4-5 Calendar
d. Growth stocks

4. In finance, _________ refers to the value of a security which is intrinsic to or contained in the security itself. It is also frequently called fundamental value. It is ordinarily calculated by summing the future income generated by the asset, and discounting it to the present value.

a. Alpha
b. Intrinsic value
c. Accretion
d. Amortization

5. _________ is a security analysis discipline for forecasting the future direction of prices through the study of past market data, primarily price and volume. In its purest form, _________ considers only the actual price and volume behavior of the market or instrument. Technical analysts may employ models and trading rules based on price and volume transformations, such as the relative strength index, moving averages, regressions, inter-market and intra-market price correlations, cycles or, classically, through recognition of chart patterns.

a. Support and resistance
b. Point and figure
c. Dow theory
d. Technical analysis

6. In options, the _________ is a key variable in a derivatives contract between two parties. Where the contract requires delivery of the underlying instrument, the trade will be at the _________, regardless of the spot price (market price) of the underlying instrument at that time.

Definition - The fixed price at which the owner of an option can purchase, in the case of a call in the case of a put, the underlying security or commodity.

a. Moneyness
b. Swaption
c. Naked put
d. Strike price

7. The _________ is one of the measures of national income and input for a given country's economy. _________ is defined as the total cost of all finished goods and services produced within the country in a stipulated period of time (usually a 365-day year.) It is sometimes regarded as the sum of profits added at every level of production (the intermediate stages) of all final goods and services produced within a country in a stipulated timeframe, and it is rarely given a monetary value.

a. Behavioral finance
b. Recession
c. Gross domestic product
d. Macroeconomics

8. In economics, a _________ is a general slowdown in economic activity in a country over a sustained period of time, or a business cycle contraction. During _________s, many macroeconomic indicators vary in a similar way. Production as measured by Gross Domestic Product (GDP), employment, investment spending, capacity utilization, household incomes and business profits all fall during _________s.

a. Behavioral finance
b. Recession
c. Mercantilism
d. Fixed exchange rate

9. The term _________ or economic cycle refers to the fluctuations of economic activity (business fluctuations) around a long-term growth trend. The cycle involves shifts over time between periods of relatively rapid growth of output (recovery and prosperity), and periods of relative stagnation or decline (contraction or recession.) These fluctuations are often measured using the real gross domestic product.
a. Fixed exchange rate
b. Behavioral finance
c. Business cycle
d. Deflation

10. _________ refers to government attempts to influence the direction of the economy through changes in government taxes, or through some spending (fiscal allowances.)

_________ can be contrasted with the other main type of economic policy, monetary policy, which attempts to stabilize the economy by controlling interest rates and the supply of money. The two main instruments of _________ are government spending and taxation.

a. Qualified residence interest
b. Fiscal policy
c. Tax exemption
d. Tax incidence

11. An _________ (or business indicator) is a statistic about the economy. _________s allow analysis of economic performance and predictions of future performance.

_________s include various indices, earnings reports, and economic summaries, such as unemployment, housing starts, Consumer Price Index (a measure for inflation), industrial production, bankruptcies, Gross Domestic Product, broadband internet penetration, retail sales, stock market prices, and money supply changes.

a. AAB
b. Economic indicator
c. A Random Walk Down Wall Street
d. ABN Amro

12. _________ is the amount by which a government, private company, or individual's spending exceeds income over a particular period of time, the opposite of budget surplus.

When the expenditures of a government to individuals and corporations) are greater than its tax revenues, it creates a deficit in the government budget; such a deficit is known as _________. This causes the government to borrow capital from the 'world market', increasing further debt, debt service and interest rates

a. 4-4-5 Calendar
b. Deficit spending
c. 7-Eleven
d. 529 plan

13. _________ is the process by which the government, or monetary authority of a country controls (i) the supply of money central bank (ii) availability of money, and (iii) cost of money or rate of interest, in order to attain a set of objectives oriented towards the growth and stability of the economy. Monetary theory provides insight into how to craft optimal _________.

_________ is referred to as either being an expansionary policy where an expansionary policy increases the total supply of money in the economy, and a contractionary policy decreases the total money supply.

a. Federal Open Market Committee
b. Tax exemption
c. Natural resources consumption tax
d. Monetary policy

14. _________ is an estimate of the fair value of corporations and their stocks, by using fundamental economic criteria. This theoretical valuation has to be perfected with market criteria, as the final purpose is to determine potential market prices.
a. 4-4-5 Calendar
b. Growth stocks
c. Security Analysis
d. Stock valuation

15. In finance, _________ is the process of estimating the potential market value of a financial asset or liability. they can be done on assets (for example, investments in marketable securities such as stocks, options, business enterprises, or intangible assets such as patents and trademarks) or on liabilities (e.g., Bonds issued by a company.) _________s are required in many contexts including investment analysis, capital budgeting, merger and acquisition transactions, financial reporting, taxable events to determine the proper tax liability, and in litigation.

a. Share
b. Margin
c. Valuation
d. Procter ' Gamble

16. _________ and the related Fisher's linear discriminant are methods used in statistics and machine learning to find the linear combination of features which best separate two or more classes of objects or events. The resulting combination may be used as a linear classifier, or, more commonly, for dimensionality reduction before later classification.

_________ is closely related to ANOVA (analysis of variance) and regression analysis, which also attempt to express one dependent variable as a linear combination of other features or measurements.

a. 4-4-5 Calendar
b. Linear discriminant analysis
c. 7-Eleven
d. 529 plan

17. _________ refers to the additional value of a commodity over the cost of commodities used to produce it from the previous stage of production. An example is the price of gasoline at the pump over the price of the oil in it. In national accounts used in macroeconomics, it refers to the contribution of the factors of production, i.e., land, labor, and capital goods, to raising the value of a product and corresponds to the incomes received by the owners of these factors.

a. Value added
b. Demand shock
c. Deregulation
d. Supply shock

18. _________ is a legal entity that develops, registers and sells securities for the purpose of financing its operations. _________s may be domestic or foreign governments, corporations or investment trusts. _________s are legally responsible for the obligations of the issue and for reporting financial conditions, material developments and any other operational activities as required by the regulations of their jurisdictions.

a. Arbitrage
b. Initial margin
c. Efficient-market hypothesis
d. Issuer

19. In business and accounting, _________s are everything of value that is owned by a person or company. The balance sheet of a firm records the monetary value of the _________s owned by the firm. The two major _________ classes are tangible _________s and intangible _________s.

a. Accounts payable
b. Income
c. EBITDA
d. Asset

20. In statistics, a _________, is a type of finite impulse response filter used to analyze a set of data points by creating a series of averages of different subsets of the full data set. A _________ is not a single number, but it is a set of numbers, each of which is the average of the corresponding subset of a larger set of data points. A _________ may also use unequal weights for each data value in the subset to emphasize particular values in the subset.
a. Moving average
b. Loans and interest, in Judaism
c. Gordon growth model
d. Voluntary Emissions Reductions

21. In finance, an _________ is the difference between the expected return of a security and the actual return. _________s are sometimes triggered by 'events.' Events can include mergers, dividend announcements, company earning announcements, interest rate increases, lawsuits, etc. all which can contribute to an _________.
a. A Random Walk Down Wall Street
b. AAB
c. ABN Amro
d. Abnormal return

22. In finance, a _________ is a security that entitles the holder to buy stock of the company that issued it at a specified price, which is usually higher than the stock price at time of issue.

_________s are frequently attached to bonds or preferred stock as a sweetener, allowing the issuer to pay lower interest rates or dividends. They can be used to enhance the yield of the bond, and make them more attractive to potential buyers.

a. Clearing house
b. Credit
c. Clearing
d. Warrant

Chapter 1

1. d	2. b	3. c	4. d	5. c	6. d	7. a	8. d	9. a	10. d

Chapter 2

1. d	2. d	3. a	4. d	5. d	6. d	7. d	8. b	9. d	10. a
11. d	12. d	13. a	14. c	15. d	16. c	17. c	18. d	19. c	20. b
21. d	22. c	23. d	24. d	25. a	26. b	27. d	28. d	29. d	30. d
31. b	32. d	33. d	34. b	35. a	36. c	37. d	38. a	39. c	40. c
41. d	42. d	43. d	44. d	45. d	46. d				

Chapter 3

1. d	2. d	3. b	4. d	5. d	6. b	7. c	8. d	9. b	10. b
11. c	12. d	13. d	14. a	15. b	16. d	17. d	18. d	19. d	

Chapter 4

1. a	2. a	3. c	4. d	5. d	6. b	7. a	8. a	9. c	10. b
11. b	12. d	13. a	14. d	15. d	16. b	17. a	18. d	19. d	20. d
21. d	22. d	23. d	24. d	25. d	26. b	27. d	28. c	29. c	30. a
31. c	32. b								

Chapter 5

1. c	2. a	3. d	4. d	5. d	6. d	7. d	8. b	9. d	10. c
11. c	12. d	13. d	14. d	15. a	16. d	17. d	18. c	19. b	20. d
21. d	22. b	23. d	24. b	25. d	26. d	27. b	28. d	29. d	

Chapter 6

1. d	2. d	3. d	4. c	5. d	6. a	7. d	8. b	9. d	10. d
11. d	12. c	13. d	14. d	15. d	16. a	17. d	18. d	19. a	20. a
21. d	22. a	23. a	24. c	25. a	26. d	27. b	28. a	29. d	30. d
31. a	32. d	33. d	34. b						

Chapter 7

1. d	2. b	3. b	4. a	5. d	6. b	7. d	8. d	9. d	10. d
11. a	12. d	13. a	14. d	15. a	16. c	17. a	18. c	19. a	20. d
21. d	22. d	23. d	24. b	25. b	26. d	27. c	28. a	29. d	30. d
31. a	32. d	33. a	34. d	35. d	36. b	37. d	38. b	39. d	40. d
41. d	42. d	43. d	44. c	45. d	46. b				

Chapter 8

1. b	2. d	3. d	4. a	5. d	6. a	7. c	8. b	9. d	10. b
11. d	12. a								

Chapter 9

1. a	2. a	3. d	4. a	5. a	6. b	7. d	8. a	9. d	10. a
11. d	12. b	13. a	14. d	15. d	16. a	17. d	18. d	19. c	20. c
21. a	22. d	23. d							

Chapter 10

1. c	2. d	3. d	4. c	5. d	6. b	7. b	8. d	9. b	10. a
11. c	12. c	13. a	14. d	15. b	16. d	17. d	18. d	19. d	20. d
21. a	22. c	23. a	24. d	25. c	26. d	27. c			

Chapter 11

1. b	2. c	3. d	4. d	5. b	6. d	7. d	8. d	9. d	10. d
11. b	12. d	13. c	14. d	15. d	16. b	17. c	18. d	19. d	20. b
21. d	22. a								

Chapter 12

1. b	2. b	3. c	4. b	5. d	6. d	7. c	8. a	9. d	10. d
11. d	12. d	13. d	14. d	15. b	16. c	17. a	18. b		

Chapter 13

1. a	2. d	3. a	4. d	5. d	6. d	7. d	8. d	9. b	10. c
11. d	12. a	13. d	14. a	15. a	16. a	17. d	18. d	19. a	20. b
21. d	22. d	23. d	24. d	25. b	26. b				

Chapter 14

1. d	2. d	3. d	4. a	5. c	6. d	7. d	8. c	9. d	10. d
11. d	12. d	13. d	14. a	15. b	16. d	17. c	18. b	19. a	20. d
21. d	22. c								

Chapter 15

1. c	2. c	3. d	4. d	5. c	6. d	7. c	8. a	9. b	10. a
11. d	12. d	13. d	14. d	15. c	16. d	17. b	18. b	19. b	20. c
21. c	22. d	23. a	24. a	25. a	26. d	27. a	28. d	29. b	30. d
31. d	32. b								

Chapter 16

1. b	2. b	3. d	4. d	5. c	6. c	7. c	8. d	9. a	10. c
11. d	12. a	13. b	14. c	15. d	16. b	17. d	18. b	19. d	20. a
21. d	22. d								

Chapter 17

1. d	2. a	3. a	4. b	5. d	6. d	7. c	8. b	9. c	10. b
11. b	12. b	13. d	14. d	15. c	16. b	17. a	18. d	19. d	20. a
21. d	22. d								

www.ingramcontent.com/pod-product-compliance
Lightning Source LLC
Chambersburg PA
CBHW082043230426
43670CB00016B/2757
9781428871601